mentor Übungsbuch

Englisch

7./8. Klasse

Die Zeiten: Bildung und Verwendung

Verena Rotter

Mit praktischem Lösungsteil zum Heraustrennen

mentor
Eine Klasse besser.

Die Autorin: Verena Rotter, Lehrerin für Englisch, Kunsterziehung, Werken und Technisches Zeichnen

Redaktion: Ulrike Timmer

Illustrationen: Henning Schöttke, Kiel

Umwelthinweis: Gedruckt auf chlorfrei gebleichtem Papier

Layout: Peter Glaubitz, auf der Basis des Layouts von Barbara Slowik, München

Printed in Germany

Inhaltsverzeichnis

Unser Tipp für alle, die noch mehr wissen wollen:

mentor Lernhilfen

Die sind Spezialisten im Erklären und machen fit fürs ganze Schuljahr!

Für Englisch in der 7./8. Klasse gibt's die Bände:

Grammatik und Wortschatz:
Vertiefung der Grundlagen, Teil 1
ISBN 3-580-63545-X

Grammatik und Wortschatz:
Vertiefung der Grundlagen, Teil 2
ISBN 3-580-63546-8

Vorwort

V

Hallo, liebe Schülerin, lieber Schüler,

du möchtest dein Englisch ein bisschen trainieren, aber möglichst schnell und ohne viel Theorie? Dann bist du hier richtig – egal, ob du dich nun generell verbessern oder eines der Themen dieses Buches speziell für eine Klassenarbeit üben willst.

Du wirst sehen – jetzt geht's besonders easy:

Treffsicher – Dieses Buch ist in **24 kleine Lernportionen** gegliedert.
→ So findest du dich besonders schnell zurecht.

Übersichtlich – Jede Lernportion umfasst genau eine **Doppelseite**.
→ So hast du immer alles auf einen Blick.

Einleuchtend – Jede Doppelseite beginnt mit einer kurzen, klaren **Regel**.
→ So weißt du immer sofort, worauf es ankommt.

Clever – Dann geht's ans **Üben** – ganz locker, Schritt für Schritt.
→ So bereitest du dich optimal vor.

Praktisch – Der **Lösungsteil** zum Heraustrennen passt seitengetreu dazu.
→ So kontrollierst du blitzschnell – ohne Suchen und Blättern.

Am besten gleich loslegen!

Viel Spaß und ganz viel Erfolg

wünscht dir

dein mentor Verlag

Noch ein Tipp – Du hast noch mehr Nachholbedarf, aber keine Lust auf Nachhilfe? Dann versuch's doch mit den **mentor Lernhilfen**: Schau mal auf die Seite gegenüber!

A Aktiv

In einem Aktivsatz ist das Subjekt des Satzes (z. B. Person, Tier, Sache) der Verursacher einer Handlung.

1. Simple Present: Bejahte Sätze

Verwendung

- für regelmäßige Handlungen → I always do my homework at 2 p.m.
- bei Tatsachenbeschreibungen → Our school is next to a park.
- bei Zustandsverben → This book belongs to Jane.

Bildung (Vollverben)

Verb in der Grundform → I like history.

bei der 3. Person Singular *(he/she/it)* wird ein *-s* angehängt → My sister likes biology.

Sonderformen in der Schreibweise (3. Pers. Sing.)

- nach *o, s, x, z, ch, sh*: + *-es* → Peter goes to grammar school.
- *y* nach Konsonant wird zu *-ie-* → Lucy cries whenever she gets a bad mark.

Merke

Signalwörter:
always, often, sometimes, never, every (week), on (Saturdays)

Übung 1

Mit *-s* oder ohne? Bilde die richtige Verbform.

The Parkers live...... in Bristol. Mr Parker work...... as a computer programmer *(dt. Programmierer)* in a big company. The Parkers have four children: Ben, Steve, Sarah and Julie. Ben, who is 17, attend...... the last year of grammar school. He want...... to go to university afterwards. His girl-friend Emma live...... in Bristol, too. She work...... in a hospital as a nurse. Sarah and Steve are twins. They are 13 years old and attend...... a big comprehensive school. Julie, who is eight, love...... going to her elementary school.

Übung 2 **Setze die richtige Verbform ein. Achte auf Sonderformen.**

Sarah and Steve .... (get up) at 7.30 on weekdays. Sarah often .... (spend) half an hour in the bathroom and then .... (hurry) to catch the bus. She says, "I really .... (love) school but my brother .... (hate) it. He only .... (like) P.E. Steve .... (play) tennis in the school team and he never .... (miss) a match on TV. My favourite teacher is Mr Harrison. He .... (come) from Newcastle and .... (teach) geography."

Übung 3 **Bilde Sätze anhand der Informationen in der Tabelle.**

	like(s)	**hate(s)**
Ben	technology	French
Steve & Sarah	P.E.	science
Julie	art	history
I	?	?

1. Ben .... technology but he .... French.
2. Steve and Sarah ....
3. Julie ....
4. I ....

Übung 4 **Bilde Sätze. Achte auf die richtige Stellung der Häufigkeitsadverbien.**

1. Ben / get up / at 7 o'clock / every morning

....

2. He / use / his motorbike / to get to school / sometimes

....

....

3. Ben / watch / films / on TV / in the evening / often

....

....

2. Simple Present: Verneinte Sätze

Bildung:	
Vollverben	
do / does + *not* + Grundform	→ I don't like our timetable.
(Kurzformen: *don't / doesn't)*	→ Jerry doesn't play in the school team.
Formen von *to be* /	
Hilfsverben	
Form von *to be* + *not*	→ My brother isn't good at maths.
Hilfsverb + *not*	→ I cannot / can't speak French.
	→ We haven't got art this year.
Beachte:	
I must ↔ I needn't	ich muss ↔ ich muss nicht
I may ↔ I mustn't	ich darf ↔ ich darf nicht

Übung 1

Verneinte Hilfsverben und Formen von *to be*.
Setze die richtigen Verbformen ein.

Sarah is good at school but she .... (not, be) the best pupil in her class.

She speaks German fairly well but she .... (not, can) speak Italian.

Her parents are happy when she gets a good mark but they .... (not, be) angry with her when she gets a bad one. Her twin brother Steve often asks her: "Do you know how to solve this maths problem?"

Mostly, Sarah's answer is, "No, I .... (not, have got) a clue."
(dt. ich habe keine Ahnung)

Sarah's favourite subject is geography but she .... (not, be) good at biology and she .... (not, can) stand physics.

She says "I really like school but I .... (not, be) a swot *(dt. Streber)*."

Übung 2

Verneinte Vollverben.
Setze die richtigen Verbformen ein.

Sarah continues: "I like German but I .... (not, like) our German teacher, Mr March. He .... (not, explain) anything at all and he .... (not, help) us when we've got a problem.

Vicky and I often .... (not, understand) a single word because he speaks so fast. He gives us loads of homework but he .... (not, correct) it. That's a shame, isn't it?

Sometimes I think that he .... (not, like) teaching at all."

Übung 3

Must, needn't, may, mustn't.
Setze die sinngemäß richtige Form ein.

1. Sarah and Steve Parker .... get up at 7.30 in the morning on weekdays but they .... stay in bed as long as they like on Saturdays and Sundays.
2. Mrs Parker always tells them to hurry in the morning because they .... miss their bus. If Steve and Sarah miss the bus, they .... go to school by bike. Last week, Sarah's bike had a puncture *(dt. einen Platten)*. Her mother said, "You .... use mine instead."
3. Mr Holden, their physics teacher, is very strict. He once said, "You .... forget to do your homework, otherwise you .... stay in school all night long." Sarah was really shocked but a friend told her: "You .... be afraid of him. He was only joking."

Übung 4

Bilde Sätze.

1. In England / school / not / begin / at eight o'clock

   ....

2. German pupils / not / have got / assembly / in the morning

   ....

   ....

3. In England / school / not / finish / at 1 p.m.

   ....

   ....

4. Very often / German pupils / not / can / have lunch / at school

   ....

   ....

3. Simple Present: Fragesätze

Im Englischen werden Fragesätze in der Regel immer mit einem Hilfsverb gebildet.

Bildung:

Vollverben

(Fragewort +) *do* / *does* + Subjekt + Grundform	→ Do you like our new maths teacher?
	→ Does Mr Stevens teach French?

Hilfsverben / Formen von *to be*

(Fragewort +) Hilfsverb + Subjekt + Grundform	→ Can you help me, please? Have you got a pencil?
(Fragewort +) Form von *to be* + Subjekt	→ Is your sister good at school?

Subjektfragen

Who / *What* / *Which* … + Simple Present (keine Umschreibung!!!)	→ Who likes English? Which subjects cause you problems?

Übung 1 **Übersetze die unterstrichenen Satzteile.**

1. Kann Sarah Julie bei der Mathehausaufgabe helfen?

   .... help Julie with her maths homework?

2. Hilft sie ihr jeden Tag?

   .... her every day?

3. Spielen Sarah und Vicky in der Schulmannschaft Tennis?

   .... tennis in the school team?

4. Sind sie gute Tennisspielerinnen?

   .... good tennis players?

5. Ist Ben gut im Schreiben von Aufsätzen?

   .... good at writing essays?

6. Schreibt er jede Woche einen Aufsatz?

   .... an essay every week?

Übung 2 **Frage nach den unterstrichenen Satzteilen.**

1. Julie gets up at 8 a.m.

....

2. Her mother makes breakfast for her.

....

3. Julie can use her bike to get to school.

....

4. Julie's schoolbag weighs two kilos.

....

5. Julie likes art.

....

Übung 3 **Steve soll für die Schülerzeitung einen neuen Lehrer, Mr Jackson, interviewen. Er hat sich schon überlegt, was er ihn fragen will ... Bilde vollständige Fragesätze.**

1. you / like / school	→ Do you
2. which subjects / you / teach	→
3. where / you / live	→
4. when / you / have to / get up / on schooldays	→
5. you / can / walk / to school	→
6. you / have / a car	→
7. you / be / married	→
8. your wife / work	→
9. have got / you / any children	→
10. how / old / you / be	→
11. you / play / tennis	→

4. Present Progressive

Verwendung

• für Handlungen, die gerade passieren	→ I'm doing my homework at the moment.

Bildung:

bejahter Satz	
am / are / is + Grundform + *-ing*	→ Julie is helping her mum.
verneinter Satz	
am / are / is + *not* + Grundform + *-ing*	→ I'm not working in the garden.
Fragesatz	
(Fragewort +) *am / are / is* + Subjekt + Grundform + *-ing*	→ Are you watching the tennis match?

Sonderformen in der Schreibweise

• stummes *-e* entfällt	→ Ben is writing an essay.
• Konsonantenverdopplung nach kurzem, betontem Vokal	→ Mr and Mrs Parker are sitting in the living-room.
• *-ie* wird zu *-y-*	→ Sarah is lying in the garden.

Merke

Signalwörter:
at the moment, now, just (now), right now, still, Look! …, Listen! …

Übung 1

Bilde zu folgenden Verben die *-ing*-Form.

get →	go →
carry →	leave →
take →	fly →
stop →	run →

Übung 2 Es ist Samstagabend. Was machen die Parkers gerade?

1. Julie .... (visit) her friend Jackie.
2. Ben and Emma .... (watch) a video.
3. Mr Parker .... (put up) a new fence.
4. Steve and his friend Eric .... (surf) the Net.
5. Mrs Parker .... (bake) a cake.
6. Sarah .... (help) her mother.

Übung 3 Vervollständige den Text mit Verbformen im Present Progressive.

Just as Mrs Parker .... (put) the cake into the oven the phone rings. "Sarah, would you please answer the phone?" she asks. Sarah lifts the receiver. "Who .... (call)?" Mrs Parker wants to know. "It's Auntie Heather." "Tell her to hang on ... I .... (come)."

Mrs Parker: Hello, Heather. How are you? ... What .... (you, do)?

Heather: Jim and I .... (sit) in the garden.

We .... (just, have) a nice cup of tea.

And what .... (go on) at your place, Kelly?

Mrs Parker: Well, my husband .... (work) in the garden.

Heather: .... (he, cut) the grass again?

Mrs Parker: No, Fred .... (put up) a new fence today.

Heather: And the kids? What .... (they, do)?

Mrs Parker: Well, Julie .... (visit) Jackie. Ben and Emma .... (lie) in front of the telly,

Steve .... (sit) in front of the computer and Sarah .... (not, do) anything special at the moment.

She .... just .... (listen to) what I .... (tell) you now."

A 5. Simple Present und Present Progressive im Vergleich

Während wir im Deutschen nur ein Präsens haben, muss man im Englischen zwischen zwei Gegenwartsformen unterscheiden:

Verwendung:

Simple Present		Present Progressive
• bei regelmäßigen, wiederkehrenden Handlungen *I get up at 7 o'clock every morning.*	↔	• bei momentanen Handlungen *I am getting up at the moment.*
• bei Tatsachenbeschreibungen *London lies on the Thames.*	↔	*Sarah is lying on the beach right now.*
• bei Zustandsverben *Steve hates science.*		

Merke

Signalwörter:

Simple Present
always, often, sometimes, never, usually, normally, every (Tuesday), on (Sundays)

Present Progressive
at the moment, now, just (now), right now, still, Look! …, Listen! …

Zustandsverben gibt es nur in der Simple Form! Hierzu gehören: *be, believe, belong, cost, forget, hate, hear, like, love, mean, remember, see, seem, smell, understand, want, wish*

Übung 1

Simple Present oder Present Progressive?

1. Ben .... (take, usually) a shower in the morning.
2. Steve often .... (play) tennis in the afternoon.
   But he .... (not, play) tennis at the moment.
   He .... (read).
3. What .... (Mrs Parker, do) right now? –
   She .... (put up) the curtains.
4. Mr Parker .... (work) in a computer firm. That's his job.
   At the moment he .... (work) in the garden.
5. Julie .... (not, tidy up) her room very often.
   She .... (hate) doing it.

Übung 2

Sarah schreibt Vicky einen Brief aus ihrem Urlaub in Schottland. Setze die richtigen Verbformen ein.

Dear Vicky,

I .... (write) this letter in a café in Inverness. Mum, Julie and I .... (sit) here and we .... (have) a nice cup of tea. The weather .... (be) fine today. We .... (get up) late every morning. Dad .... (get up) first and .... (make) breakfast for us. After breakfast we usually .... (go walking). Ben sometimes .... (use) his mountain bike to get up the hills. The countryside .... (be) beautiful and I simply .... (love) these Highland cattle – you .... (know), the ones with the long hair. Mum and Julie .... (leave) now. Gotta go!

See you soon. Love, Sarah

Übung 3

Die Parkers sind zum Loch Ness gefahren. Übersetze ins Englische.

Julie: Dad, was weißt du über Nessie?

....

Mr Parker: Frag Steve. Er liest gerade ein Buch über Nessie.

....

Julie: Steve, glaubst du, dass Nessie wirklich hier lebt?

....

Steve: Ich weiß nicht. Schau mal! Da drüben bewegt sich was ...

....

....

A 6. Simple Past: Bejahte Sätze

Verwendung
- für abgeschlossene Ereignisse in der Vergangenheit → The Parkers spent their holiday in Scotland.

Bildung:
regelmäßig
Grundform + *-ed* → They enjoyed their holiday very much.
unregelmäßig
2. Form des Verbs → They came back last night.

Sonderformen in der Schreibweise
- stummes *-e* entfällt → The Parkers arrived at 8.30 p.m.
- Konsonantenverdopplung nach kurzem, betontem Vokal → They stopped at the front door.
- *y* nach Konsonant wird zu *-i-* → Mr Parker carried the heavy suitcases into the house.

Merke

Signalwörter:
yesterday, last (week), (2 years) ago, in (1993), when?

Übung 1

Regelmäßig oder unregelmäßig?
Wie lautet das Simple Past der folgenden Verben?

to buy →	to write →
to drive →	to return →
to travel →	to say →
to send →	to tell →

Übung 2 **Nach seiner Rückkehr ruft Ben Emma an. Ergänze den Dialog.**

Ben: Hi, Emma! I'm back.

Emma: Hello, dear! I .... (miss) you. Did you enjoy your holiday?

Ben: Of course I .... (do). The weather .... (be) nice and we .... (have) a lot of fun – well, most of the time …
Actually, I .... (break) my right arm three days ago.

Emma: Oh dear! What happened?

Ben: I simply .... (fall) off my bike when I was going down a bumpy road. My father .... (take) me to hospital.
The doctors there .... (put) my arm in plaster *(dt. Gips)*.

Übung 3 **Sarah und Vicky zeigen sich ihre Tagebücher. Was haben sie z. B. am 27. August erlebt? Ergänze die fehlenden Verbformen.**

Sarah's diary:

We .... (leave) Glasgow at 8 a.m. Dad .... (drive) all the way to Perth. In the afternoon we .... (arrive) at our holiday flat. It .... (look) awful. Mum and I .... (have to) clean the floor first. Julie and Steve .... (wash) the dirty dishes and Dad and Ben .... (go) shopping, because we .... (need) some food for dinner. After dinner we .... (watch) a funny film on TV.

Vicky's diary:

I .... (sleep) till 10 o'clock this morning. After breakfast I .... (help) Mum with the shopping.
In the afternoon it .... (get) really hot, so Karen and I .... (decide) to go swimming. Today we .... (swim) a mile in less than an hour. Dad .... (be) really proud of me when he .... (hear) about it. Karen and I .... (be) extremely tired afterwards, so we .... (spend) the rest of the day in the garden lying lazily in the sun …

A 7. Simple Past: Verneinte Sätze und Fragesätze

a) Verneinter Satz:

Vollverben

did + *not* + Grundform (Kurzform: *didn't*)	→ Sarah didn't go swimming in Scotland.

Formen von *to be*

was / *were* + *not* (Kurzformen: *wasn't* / *weren't*)	→ The weather wasn't always nice.

b) Fragesatz:

Vollverben

(Fragewort +) *did* + Subjekt + Grundform	→ Did you enjoy your holiday? Which places did you visit?

Formen von *to be*

(Fragewort +) *was* / *were* + Subjekt	→ Was the journey boring? What was the weather like?

Subjektfragen

who / *which* etc. + Simple Past (keine Umschreibung mit *did*!)	→ Who went to Scotland?

Übung 1

**Berichtige die „Falschaussagen".
Setze die richtigen Verbformen ein.**

1. The Parkers were *in Wales* last week.

   No, they .... (not, be) in Wales. They were in Scotland.

2. The Parkers went *by train*.

   No, they .... (not, go) by train. They went by car.

3. The Parkers stayed *in a hotel* in Perth.

   No, they .... (not, stay) in a hotel. They stayed in a holiday flat.

4. Sarah saw lots of *kangaroos* in Scotland.

   No, she .... (not, see) kangaroos. She saw Highland cattle.

5. Ben broke his *leg* in Scotland.

   No, Ben .... (not, break) his leg. He broke his arm.

6. Julie was *happy* when they left Scotland.

   No, she .... (not, be) happy. She was sad.

Übung 2

Sarah trifft sich mit ihrer Freundin Karen. Diese will einiges über Sarahs Urlaub wissen. Bilde Fragesätze im Simple Past.

1. weather / be / nice / in Scotland

   ....

2. where / you / stay

   ....

3. you / see / Nessie

   ....

4. who / take / Ben / to hospital

   ....

5. when / you / return

   ....

Übung 3

Sarah hat einen Brief von Laura, ihrer deutschen Brieffreundin, bekommen. Kannst du ihn ihr übersetzen?

Hallo Sarah,

wie war euer Urlaub?

....

Hat dir Schottland gefallen?

....

Hast du *Highland cattle* gesehen?

....

Wir sind nicht in Urlaub gefahren, weil meine Eltern nicht genug Geld hatten.

....

....

Aber ich war nicht traurig, weil das Wetter hier auch schön war.

....

....

Schreib mir bitte bald! Laura

.... Laura

A 8. Past Progressive

Verwendung

- für Handlungsabläufe

a) zu einem Zeitpunkt oder → Yesterday at 3 p.m. I was working.

b) innerhalb eines Zeitraums in der Vergangenheit → Between 6 p.m. and 7 p.m. the Parkers were having dinner.

Bildung:

bejahter Satz

was / were + Grundform + *-ing* → Ben and Emma were watching TV all night long.

verneinter Satz

was / were + *not* + Grundform + *-ing* → Steve wasn't watching TV.

Fragesatz

(Fragewort +) *was / were* + Subjekt + Grundform + *-ing* → Was Julie doing her homework at 1 p.m.?

Merke

Signalwörter:
yesterday at (8) o'clock, between (1 p.m.) and (2 p.m.) yesterday, last (week), while

Übung 1

Was haben die Parkers gestern um 16 Uhr gemacht?

1. Mr Parker .... (have) a meeting with colleagues.
2. Mrs Parker .... (buy) some clothes.
3. Steve and Eric .... (play) tennis.
4. Ben .... (repair) his motorbike.
5. Julie .... (do) her homework.
6. Sarah and Vicky .... (sit) in front of the telly.

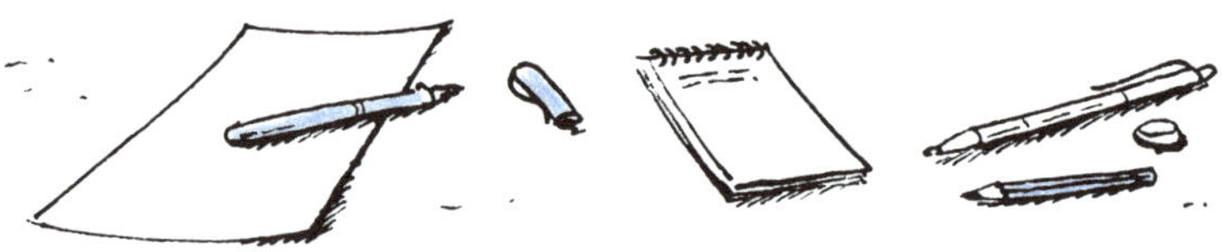

Übung 2

Gestern Abend war Großputz bei den Parkers. Was haben sie zwischen 18 und 20 Uhr gemacht?

While Mr Parker .... (scrub) the floor, Mrs Parker .... (vacuum, *dt. staubsaugen*). Sarah and Steve .... (take down) the curtains, while Julie .... (wipe out) the cupboards. Mrs Parker's sister Heather .... (help), too. She .... (clean) the windows. Ben was the only one who .... (not, work). He .... (lie) on the sofa the whole time, because he still had his arm in plaster.

Übung 3

Die Parkers sehen sich einen Krimi an. Inspector Fox befragt gerade einige Personen, was sie zur Zeit des Banküberfalls gemacht haben. Setze die richtigen Verbformen ein.

Inspector: Well, Mr Hunter, what .... (you, do) yesterday at 4 p.m.?

Mr Hunter: I .... (work).

Inspector: Where .... (you, work)?

Mr Hunter: I .... just .... (sell) a brand-new car in my shop.

Inspector: And you, Mr Thomas? What .... (you, do) at the time the robbery took place?

Mr Thomas: Of course I .... (not, rob) the bank. My wife and I .... (walk) our dog Jessie between 3.30 and 4 o'clock. Then we met some friends and we .... (have) tea with them till 5 p.m.

Inspector: What about you, Mrs Oldham? What .... (you, do) yesterday at 4 p.m.?

Mrs Oldham: Well, at 4 p.m. I .... (chat) to my neighbour, Mrs Donovan. We .... (sit) in her living-room. She can testify *(dt. bezeugen)* to this, of course. You know, we .... (talk) about …

Inspector: Thank you, Mrs Oldham, that's enough for the moment …

9. Simple Past und Past Progressive im Vergleich

Verwendung:

Simple Past

- für einmalige oder wiederholte, abgeschlossene Ereignisse in der Vergangenheit.
- bei Zustandsverben

Last week Sarah got up at 9 o'clock every day. ↔

Past Progressive

- für Handlungsabläufe zu einem bestimmten Zeitpunkt oder Zeitraum in der Vergangenheit.

Yesterday she was still sleeping at 9 a.m.

Merke

Signalwörter:

Simple Past

when, suddenly, last (week), (three days) ago, yesterday

Past Progressive

while, vergangene Zeitpunkte und Zeiträume

Kommen in einem Satz mehrere Verben im Past Tense vor, verwendet man:

nur Simple Past

- bei kurz aufeinander folgenden Ereignissen in der Vergangenheit

When the alarm clock rang, Sarah got up and rushed downstairs. ↔

nur Past Progressive

- bei mehreren Handlungen in der Vergangenheit, die gleichzeitig stattfanden

While Steve and Julie were playing cards, Mrs Parker was clearing the table.

Simple Past und Past Progressive

- wenn eine nicht abgeschlossene Handlung in der Vergangenheit (→ Past Progressive) von einem neuen Ereignis (→ Simple Past) unterbrochen wurde

Sarah was reading a girls' magazine when suddenly the door opened and her mother came in.

Übung 1 **Julie ist im Schulhof hingefallen. Zu Hause berichtet sie davon ... Welche Past Tense Form passt hier?**

"I don't know how it .... (happen). I suddenly .... (stumble, *dt. stolpern*) and .... (fall down). My left knee bled *(dt. blutete)*. It really .... (hurt) but I .... (not, cry). Jackie, who .... (see) me lying on the ground, ... (come) to me at once. Then she .... (send) Daniel to look for a teacher. Mrs Bell, who .... (be) there within two minutes, ... (have) a first-aid kit with her. First she .... (put) a bandage on my knee. Then she .... (go) to our maths teacher, Mr Collins, and .... (tell) him that I .... (need) some rest. That's why I .... (not, must) write the maths test today ... Wasn't I lucky?"

Übung 2 **Steve und seine Freunde verbrachten gestern einen Nachmittag am Strand ... Was haben sie gemacht?**

1. Steve and Eric / buy some soft drinks, Tom / get some crackers

   While Steve and Eric .... some soft drinks,

   Tom .... some crackers.

2. Justin / look for a place for the camp fire, Dave / collect some wood

   While ....

   ....

3. everybody else / sunbathe *(dt. sonnenbaden)*, Joe and Paul / build a big sandcastle

   While ....

   ....

Übung 3 **Der Tag am Strand verlief nicht ganz ungestört. Was passierte plötzlich? Verwende die geeigneten Past Tense Formen.**

1. While Steve .... (carry) ten cans of lemonade, a ball .... (hit) his head and he .... (drop) the cans.
2. A mosquito .... (bite) Dave while he .... (collect) wood for the camp fire.
3. While Joe and Paul .... (build) the sandcastle, a big wave suddenly .... (come) and .... (wash) it away.

A 10. Present Perfect Simple

Das Present Perfect ist eine Zeitform, die eine Verbindung von der Vergangenheit zur Gegenwart herstellt.
Es ist daher **nicht** mit dem deutschen Perfekt gleichzusetzen.

Verwendung
für Ereignisse, die

- in der Vergangenheit begannen und noch andauern → Ben has known Emma for three years.
- gerade abgeschlossen wurden → Steve and Sarah have just left.
- abgeschlossen sind, aber Auswirkungen auf die Gegenwart haben → Julie has cleaned her shoes. (They are clean now.)
- in der Vergangenheit (nicht) stattfanden; es wird aber keine Zeitangabe genannt → The Parkers have been to Wales twice but they've never been to Ireland.

Bildung:
bejahter Satz
have / has + 3. Form des Verbs → He has just gone to work.
verneinter Satz
have / has + *not* + 3. Form (Kurzformen: *haven't / hasn't*) → Steve and Sarah haven't done their homework yet.
Fragesatz
(Fragewort +) *have / has* + Subjekt + 3. Form → Has Julie cleaned her room yet?

Merke

Signalwörter:
just, (not) yet, already, since (für Zeitpunkte), ***for*** (für Zeiträume), ***so far, up to now, ever, never, today, this morning / week …*** (wenn dieser Zeitraum schon begonnen hat, aber noch nicht vorbei ist)

Übung 1

Zeitpunkt oder Zeitraum? Setze *since* bzw. *for* ein.

1. Mr and Mrs Parker have known each other .... 1980.
2. The Parkers have lived in their house .... more than 17 years now.
3. Steve hasn't had a haircut .... a long time.
4. Sarah hasn't seen her grandparents .... last Christmas.
5. Julie hasn't tidied up her room .... three weeks.

Übung 2

Bevor Steve, Sarah und Julie weggehen, will ihre Mutter wissen, ob sie schon ihre Aufgaben erledigt haben …

Mrs Parker: Sarah, ... (you, do) the washing up?

Sarah: It's Steve's turn today. But as far as I know, he .... (not, wash) the dishes yet.

Mrs Parker: Steve, why .... (you, not, do) the washing up?

Steve: I'm sorry, I forgot. But look, I .... (clear) the table and I .... (put) most of the stuff into the dishwasher. I'll do the washing up later …

Mrs Parker: No, you won't. You've got to do it now. – Where is Julie? Juuuuuuuliiiieeee!!!! .... (you, tidy up) your room yet? It looked awful this morning! … *(no answer)*

Sarah: Perhaps she .... (leave, already).
But she .... (tidy up) her room.
I .... (just, see) it. It looks great now …

Übung 3

Diesmal will Laura Sarah einen Brief auf Englisch schreiben. Hilfst du ihr?

Dear Sarah,

I .... (not, hear) from you for three weeks. Are you still alive? I can't wait to hear about your holiday in Scotland. Unfortunately, I .... (never, be) to Scotland. Wales must be great, too. .... (you, ever, be) there? Although we .... (not, be) away on holiday this year, I didn't get bored. I .... (just, take up) riding. I .... (have) two lessons so far. .... (you, ever, ride) a horse? I think it's wonderful … Write soon. Love, Laura

A 11. Present Perfect Progressive

Verwendung
für Handlungen, die

- in der Vergangenheit anfingen und bis (oder fast bis) in die Gegenwart reichen → Steve has been playing tennis since two o'clock.
- gerade abgeschlossen sind, aber Auswirkungen auf die Gegenwart haben → Julie and Sarah have been inline-skating. (They are completely exhausted now.)

Bildung:
bejahter Satz
has / have + *been* + Grundform + *-ing* → I have been dancing all night.
verneinter Satz
has / have + *not* + *been* + Grundform + *-ing* → Mr Parker hasn't been working today.
(Kurzformen: *haven't / hasn't)*
Fragesatz
(Fragewort +) *has / have* + Subjekt + *been* + Grundform + *-ing* → How long has Steve been playing tennis?

Merke

Signalwörter:
for (für Zeiträume), ***since*** (für Zeitpunkte), ***all (day / night ...)***, ***how long?***

Übung 1

Was machen die Parkers seit heute Morgen? Setze die richtige Verbform ein.

1. Mr and Mrs Parker .... (garden, *dt. im Garten arbeiten*) all day.
2. Steve .... (play) games on his computer.
3. Julie .... (walk) her friend's dog since 7 a.m.
4. Ben .... (lie) on his bed for three hours.
5. Sarah .... (sit) on a bench in the garden all day. She and Vicky .... (talk) to each other on the phone since 11 a.m.

Übung 2

Als Sarah und Steve abends nach Hause kommen, will ihre Mutter wissen, was sie den ganzen Tag gemacht haben.

Mrs Parker: Hello Steve, how was your day?

Steve: I'm exhausted Mum. I .... (play) basketball since 2 p.m. I'm really shattered *(dt. erledigt)* now …

Mrs Parker: And what about you, Sarah? What .... (you, do) all afternoon?

Sarah: Vicky and I .... (chat) on the Net with two German students, Lars and Nick. What about your day, Mum? .... (you, work) hard today?

Mrs Parker: Well, I .... (wash) clothes all day.

Sarah: What about Dad and Ben?

Mrs Parker: Ben .... (write) letters since 1 p.m. and Dad .... (try) to repair the toaster …

Übung 3

Kannst du zwischen Sarah und Lars dolmetschen?

English	German
Sarah: How long have you and Nick been chatting on the Net today?	
	Lars: Wir chatten seit zwei Stunden.
Sarah: How long have you and Nick been learning English?	
	Lars: Wir lernen seit acht Jahren Englisch. Nick studiert Englisch seit zwei Jahren.

A 12. Present Perfect Simple und Present Perfect Progressive im Vergleich

Present Perfect Simple und Present Perfect Progressive stellen eine Verbindung von der Vergangenheit zur Gegenwart her.
Beachte aber die Unterschiede in der Verwendung:

Present Perfect Simple		**Present Perfect Progressive**
• betont das Ergebnis einer Handlung *Julie has cleaned her shoes. They look great now.*	↔	• betont die Dauer einer Handlung *Mrs Parker has been cleaning shoes for two hours.*
• steht in Verbindung mit *how much?* bzw. *how many?* *Ben has written five letters.*	↔	• steht in Verbindung mit *how long?* *Ben has been writing letters since 1 p.m.*
• bei Zustandsverben *Steve has known Eric for eight years.*	↔	• bei Tätigkeitsverben *Steve and Eric have been inline-skating for three hours.*

Merke

Signalwörter:

Present Perfect Simple
how many?, how much?, so far, up to now, already, (not) yet, ever, never, this week, since, for, how long? mit Zustandsverb

Present Perfect Progressive
all day, all night, since, for, how long? mit Tätigkeitsverb

Übung 1

Zustandsverb oder Tätigkeitsverb?
Verwende die richtige Present Perfect Form.

1. Steve .... (have) his computer for three years.
2. He .... (play) computer games for 30 minutes now.
3. Ben and Emma .... (be) together for a long time.
4. Vicky and Sarah .... (deliver) newspapers all day.
5. Julie .... (draw) a picture since 1 p.m.
6. She .... (love) art ever since her first lesson in it.

Übung 2

Mrs Parker telefoniert mit ihrer Schwester Heather. Wähle die passenden Present Perfect Formen.

Mrs Parker: Hello, Heather, what .... (you, do) all day?

Heather: I .... (garden) since 10 a.m.

I .... (plant) new trees and bushes.

Mrs Parker: That sounds great. I .... (not, plant) trees for years. How many .... (you, plant) so far?

Heather: About twenty. And what .... (you, do) on such a beautiful day?

Mrs Parker: Well, I .... (bake) cakes all day for Julie's birthday party. We .... (not, have) a big party for a long time …

Übung 3

Bilde aus den Wörtern Sätze. Entscheide, ob die Dauer oder das Ergebnis der Handlung betont ist.

1. Mr Parker and his brother Mike / catch / fish / all day

....

....

2. Ben / not / read / a single book / today

....

3. Vicky and Sarah / know each other / for years

....

4. Mr Collins / correct / the maths tests / all afternoon

....

....

5. Laura / ever / be / to Scotland / ?

....

13. Past Tense und Present Perfect im Vergleich

Während im Deutschen das Imperfekt und das Perfekt ohne Bedeutungsunterschied ausgetauscht werden können, ist dies im Englischen nicht möglich. Man verwendet:

Past Tense

- für Ereignisse, die in der Vergangenheit stattfanden und abgeschlossen sind
  Ben met Emma yesterday. ↔
- wenn eine Zeitangabe in der Vergangenheit gemacht wird (der Zeitpunkt ist wichtig)
  The Parkers were in Scotland last month. ↔

Present Perfect

- für Ereignisse, die in der Vergangenheit begannen und noch nicht abgeschlossen sind
  They have already met three times this week.
- für vergangene Geschehnisse, die Auswirkungen auf die Gegenwart haben
  → *Ben has lost his key. (He can't get into the house now.)*
- wenn keine Zeitangabe gemacht wird („bis jetzt") (der Zeitpunkt ist unwichtig)
  They've been to Scotland many times.

Merke

Signalwörter:

Past Tense
when?, while, yesterday, last (Monday), (two weeks) ago, in (1986), while

Present Perfect
ever, never, since, for, already, (not) yet, so far, up to now, this (year), all day / night, how long? how much?, how many?

Übung 1

Setze die richtigen Verbformen ein.

	Simple Past	Present Perfect Simple
work	he	he
not / go	I	I
arrive	they	they
not / see	you	you
not / talk	she	she

Übung 2

Simple Past oder Present Perfect Simple?
Setze die richtige Verbform ein.

1. Sarah .... (receive, *dt. bekommen*) three letters this month.
2. Two days ago she .... (get) a very long letter from Laura.
3. Steve and Sarah .... (write) four tests this week.
4. The maths test last Tuesday .... (be) the most difficult one.
6. Mr Parker .... (marry) his wife in 1981.
5. They .... (be married) for a long time now.

Übung 3

Übersetze den Dialog ins Englische.
Verwende Simple Past oder Present Perfect Simple.

Vicky:	Hi, Sarah. Was hast du gestern Abend gemacht?	→ Vicky:	....
Sarah:	Ich bin auf Peters Party gegangen. – Warum bist du nicht gekommen?	→ Sarah:	....
Vicky:	Peter hat mich nicht eingeladen. – War's gut?	→ Vicky:	....
Sarah:	Es war toll. Ich habe Sam wieder getroffen. Wir kennen uns seit zwei Wochen. Hast du Sam schon mal gesehen?	→ Sarah:	....
Vicky:	Nein, ich hab ihn nie gesehen.	→ Vicky:	....

14. Past Tense und Present Perfect: Simple und Progressive Forms

Verwendung:

Simple Past
- für abgeschlossene Ereignisse in der Vergangenheit
- bei Zustandsverben

Present Perfect Simple
- wenn eine Verbindung zwischen Vergangenheit und Gegenwart besteht
- wenn das Ergebnis betont ist
- bei Zustandsverben

Past Progressive
- für abgeschlossene Handlungsabläufe in der Vergangenheit
- nur bei Tätigkeitsverben!

Present Perfect Progressive
- wenn eine Verbindung zwischen Vergangenheit und Gegenwart besteht
- wenn die Dauer betont ist
- nur bei Tätigkeitsverben!

Merke

Signalwörter:

Simple Past
when, two weeks ago, last year, yesterday

Present Perfect Simple
since, for, so far, up to now, yet, just, already, ever, never, this (week), how many?, how much?

Past Progressive
while, yesterday at … o'clock, / between … and … o'clock, last …

Present Perfect Progressive
since, for, all (day / night, …), how long?

Übung 1

Trage die Verbformen an der richtigen Stelle der Tabellen ein.

he was singing, I have swum, you haven't seen, we were celebrating, I didn't go, they were jumping, she hasn't been walking, we weren't, it started, he has been, I noticed, they have been playing, have you started, what were you doing, we have begun, she has been teasing, they carried, we haven't been talking, I was sitting, have you been lying

Simple Past	Present Perfect Simple

Past Progressive	Present Perfect Progressive

Übung 2

Tante Heather ruft Julie am Abend ihres Geburtstags an. Setze die passenden Zeitformen ein.

Heather: Hello, darling, many happy returns of the day!

What .... (you, do) all day?

Julie: Well, I .... (not, sleep) late (to sleep late, *dt. lange schlafen*) this morning.

I .... (get up) quite early. When I .... (come) downstairs, Mum and Dad .... (still, wrap) some of my birthday presents.

Heather: What .... (you, get) for your birthday, then?

Julie: I .... (get) a brand-new *Glamour Barbie* and a fantastic cake.

Steve and Sarah .... (give) me some coloured pencils and I .... (receive, *dt. bekommen*) a colouring book from Ben.

Heather: .... (have) a birthday party in the afternoon?

Julie: Well, it isn't over yet. We .... (celebrate) for five hours now. We .... (play) lots of different games and we .... (already, eat up) four cakes …

15. Past Perfect Simple und Progressive

Verwendung:

Past Perfect Simple		**Past Perfect Progressive**
• für Ereignisse, die noch vor einem Zeitpunkt in der Vergangenheit (Past Tense) stattfanden *Julie had already tidied up her room before she went out.*	↔	• für Handlungen, die (fast) bis zu einem bestimmten Zeitpunkt in der Vergangenheit (Past Tense) andauerten *Steve was tired. He had been playing tennis for two hours.*
• wenn das Ergebnis betont wird		• wenn die Dauer betont wird
• bei Zustandsverben		• bei Tätigkeitsverben

Bildung:

bejahter Satz		**bejahter Satz**
had + 3. Form (Past Participle)		*had* + *been* + Grundform + *-ing*
Steve had played tennis …	↔	*He had been playing tennis …*
verneinter Satz		**verneinter Satz**
had + *not* + 3. Form (Kurzform: *hadn't*)		*had* + *not* + *been* + Grundform + *-ing*
Julie hadn't cleaned her room …	↔	*She hadn't been cleaning it …*
Fragesatz		**Fragesatz**
(Fragewort +) *had* + Subjekt + 3. Form		(Fragewort +) *had* + Subjekt + *been* + Grundform + *-ing*
Had the film already begun …?	↔	*Had Ben been having a bath …?*

Merke

Signalwörter:

Past Perfect Simple
after, since, for, how many?, how much?

Past Perfect Progressive
after, for, since, how long?

Übung 1

Verbinde die Satzhälften zu sinnvollen Sätzen.

1. After Steve had been sunbathing for hours
2. Julie's room had looked a mess
3. After she had been writing for three hours
4. Julie began to unwrap her presents
5. After the children had been playing for five hours
6. Jackie felt sick

a) Sarah's right hand started to hurt.
b) after she had eaten four pieces of cake.
c) they got tired.
d) before she cleaned it.
e) after she had thanked everybody.
f) his skin turned red.

Übung 2 **Bilde zu den Verben das Past Perfect.**

	Simple Form	Progressive Form
sit *(bejaht)*	they	you ....
watch *(verneint)*	we	she ....
drink *(verneint)*	I	it ....
call *(Frage)*	.... you ....?	.... he ....?

Übung 3 **Zustand oder Tätigkeit? Wähle die passende Verbform.**

1. After they .... (talk) for hours, Vicky and Sarah finally fell asleep.
2. Before they got married, Mr and Mrs Parker .... (know) each other for a long time.
3. After Ben .... (have) the plaster on his arm for three weeks, the doctors removed it.
4. After she .... (wash) dirty clothes all day, Mrs Parker got sick of all the housework.

Übung 4 **Übersetze die unterstrichenen Satzteile.**

1. Nachdem Herr Parker aufgestanden war, duschte er.

   ...., he took a shower.

2. Nachdem er gefrühstückt hatte, fuhr er zur Arbeit.

   ...., he drove to work.

3. Nachdem er acht Stunden lang gearbeitet hatte, machte er Feierabend.

   ....

   ...., he called it a day.

A 16. Past Tense und Past Perfect im Vergleich

Das Past Perfect wird im Englischen nur verwendet, wenn man eine Vorzeitigkeit in Bezug auf die einfache Vergangenheit ausdrücken will. Man benutzt:

Past Perfect
- für das Geschehen, das zuerst passierte **(1st action)** *After she had cleaned her room,*

Past Tense
- für das Ereignis, das danach passierte **(2nd action)** *Sarah went swimming.*

Simple Form
- wenn das Ergebnis betont wird
- bei Zustandsverben

Progressive Form
- wenn die Dauer betont wird
- bei Tätigkeitsverben

In Verbindung mit dem Past Perfect wird nur das **Simple Past** verwendet.

Merke

Signalwörter:

Past Perfect Simple
after, since, for, how many, how much

Past Perfect Progressive
after, since, for, how long

Simple Past
before am Satzanfang (dt. bevor), *when*

Übung 1

Mrs Parker hatte gestern eine Menge zu tun.
Verwende Past Perfect Simple und Simple Past.

wake up the kids, prepare *(dt. vorbereiten)* breakfast, clear the table *(dt. den Tisch abräumen)*, wash the dishes, clean the windows, tidy up the rooms, go shopping, make dinner, iron fifteen shirts, go to bed

1. After she .... the kids, she .... breakfast.
2. After she .... the table, she .... the dishes.
3. After she .... the windows, she .... the rooms.
4. After she .... shopping, she .... dinner.
5. After she .... fifteen shirts, she .... to bed.

Übung 2 **Bilde Sätze anhand der Informationen in der Tabelle.**

	1st action	2nd action
Ben	do his homework	go to the cinema
Julie & Jackie	go swimming	visit a friend
Sarah	read a comic	call Vicky
Steve	play tennis	take a shower

1. After Ben .... his homework, he .... to the cinema.
2. Before Julie and Jackie ....,
   they ....
3. Before Sarah ....,
   she ....
4. After Steve ....,
   he ....

Übung 3 **Hilfst du Laura, den Brief zu übersetzen? Verwende Past Perfect Simple / Progressive und Simple Past.**

Liebe Sarah,	Dear Sarah,
gestern war ein furchtbarer Tag.	Yesterday .... day.
Ich wollte frühstücken, aber mein Bruder hatte bereits meine Cornflakes aufgegessen.	I .... breakfast, but my brother .... already .... my cornflakes.
Als ich zur Bushaltestelle kam, war der Bus schon abgefahren.	When I .... to the bus-stop, the bus ....
Nachdem ich 45 Minuten gegangen war, kam ich endlich an der Schule an. Aber die 1. Stunde hatte schon (längst) angefangen …	After I .... for 45 minutes, I finally .... at school. But the first lesson .... …

B Passiv

Das Passiv drückt aus, was mit einer Person oder Sache geschieht. Die Umwandlung von einem Aktiv- in einen Passivsatz ist möglich, wenn der Aktivsatz über ein Objekt verfügt.
Das Objekt des Aktivsatzes wird zum Subjekt des Passivsatzes.

Mrs Parker **Subject**	*does* **Verb (active)**	*the housework.* **Object**
The housework **Subject**	*is done* **Verb (passive)**	*by Mrs Parker.* **by + Object**

Die englische Präposition *by* entspricht dem deutschen *von*.
Ist der Verursacher der Handlung unbekannt oder nicht von Bedeutung, entfällt der so genannte *by-agent (by + Object)*.

1. Simple Present

Verwendung / Signalwörter → *siehe Aktivform, Kap. 1, S. 6*

Bildung:

bejahter Satz
am / are / is + 3. Form → The kitchen and bathroom are cleaned daily.

verneinter Satz
am / are / is + *not* + 3. Form → The washing isn't done by Mr Parker.

Fragesatz
(Fragewort +) *am / are / is* + Subjekt + 3. Form → Is your bed made every day?

Übung 1

Mrs Parker träumt oft von Mr X, einem guten Geist, der all die lästige Hausarbeit erledigt. Bilde Passivsätze mit *by-agent*.

Mr X prepares breakfast. → Breakfast ....

Mr X makes the beds. → The beds ....

Mr X washes the dishes. → The dishes ....

Mr X does the shopping. → The shopping ....

Mr X serves dinner. → Dinner ....

Übung 2

**Leider scheint es den guten Geist Mr X nicht zu geben …
Bilde Fragen und Verneinungen im Simple Present Passive.**

1. breakfast / prepare / by Mr X? ....

   No, it .... (not, prepare) by Mr X, but by Mrs Parker.

2. beds / make / by Mr X? ....

   No, they .... (not, make) by Mr X, but by Mrs Parker.

3. dishes / wash / by Mr X? ....

   No, they .... (not, wash) by Mr X, but by Mrs Parker.

4. shopping / do / by Mr X? ....

   No, it .... (not, do) by Mr X, but by Mrs Parker.

5. dinner / serve / by Mr X? ....

   No, it .... (not, serve) by Mr X, but by Mrs Parker.

Übung 3

Wandle die unterstrichenen Aktivsätze in Passivsätze mit *by-agent* um.

1. Steve is really good at playing tennis. <u>Eric never beats him</u>.

   ....

2. Julie loves art. <u>She draws beautiful pictures</u>.

   ....

3. Mr Parker's brother Mike is a car mechanic. <u>Mike usually repairs the Parkers' car</u>.

   ....

4. Ben likes technology. <u>Lenny often asks him for help</u>.

   ....

5. Sarah and Vicky are very popular. <u>Their classmates always invite them to parties</u>.

   ....

   ....

B 2. Simple Past

Verwendung / Signalwörter	→ *siehe Aktivform, Kap. 6, S. 16*
Bildung:	
bejahter Satz *was / were* + 3. Form	→ Steve and Sarah were born 13 years ago.
verneinter Satz *was / were* + *not* + 3. Form	→ The *Mona Lisa* wasn't painted by Picasso.
Fragesatz (Fragewort +) *was / were* + Subjekt + 3. Form	→ When was the Parkers' house built?

Übung 1

Gestern hatten die Parkers ihr Auto bei Mike in der Reparatur. Was wurde alles gemacht? Bilde Passivsätze im Simple Past.

oil / check, new battery / put in, brake fluid *(dt. Bremsflüssigkeit)* / refill, one outside mirror and windscreen / replace, indicators *(dt. Blinker)* / repair, CD player / install, the whole car / clean

1. The oil ....
2. A new battery ....
3. The brake fluid ....
4. One outside mirror and the windscreen ....
5. The ....
6. A ....
7. Finally the whole ....

Übung 2

Hier kannst du deine Allgemeinbildung testen!
Bilde aus den Wörtern in der Tabelle die richtigen Passivsätze.
Verwende den *by-agent*, falls nötig.

America	bear (bore, born) *(dt. gebären)*	in World War II.
The *Mona Lisa*	defeat *(dt. besiegen)*	Columbus in 1492.
Neuschwanstein	write	in the 19th century.
Goethe	discover	Leonardo da Vinci.
Germany	build	in 1749.
The *Odyssey*	paint	Homer.

1. America ......

2. The *Mona Lisa* ......

3. *Neuschwanstein* ......

4. Goethe ......

5. Germany ......

6. The *Odyssey* ......

Übung 3

Wissen deine Eltern oder Freunde die richtigen Daten? Frage sie und korrigiere sie, falls sie falsche Antworten geben.

1. When ...... (Goethe, bear)?

   No, he ...... (not, bear) in …, he was born in …

2. When ...... (America, discover)?

   No, it ...... (not, discover) in …, but in …

3. When ...... (Neuschwanstein, build)? – No, it ...... (not, build) in …, it was built in …

Übung 4

Sarah war in York und schreibt nun Laura etwas über diese Stadt und die Wikinger. Übersetze ins Deutsche.

Britain was invaded by the Vikings *(dt. Wikinger)* about 1200 years ago. York was called Jorvik by the Vikings. The Vikings also landed in France where they were called Normans *(dt. Normannen)*. In 1066 King Harold II was defeated and killed in the Battle of Hastings by the Norman William the Conqueror.	Vor ungefähr 1200 Jahren ......

3. Present Perfect Simple

Verwendung / Signalwörter → *siehe Aktivform, Kap. 10, S. 24*

Bildung:
bejahter Satz
have / has + *been* + 3. Form → The kitchen has been cleaned.
verneinter Satz
have / has + *not* + *been* + 3. Form → The trees haven't been cut this year.
Fragesatz
(Fragewort +) *have / has* + Subjekt + *been* + 3. Form → Has the car been tanked up?

Übung 1

Als Mr Parker das Auto aus der Reparatur holt, will er wissen, ob auch alles erledigt worden ist. Bilde Frage- und Antwortsätze im Present Perfect Simple Passive.

Mr Parker: Hi, Mike. Is the car okay again?

Mike: Yes, of course.

Mr Parker: .... (oil, check)?

Mike: Yes, it .... (check).

Mr Parker: What about the brake fluid?
.... (it, refill)?

Mike: Certainly.

Mr Parker: And the mirror and the windscreen …
.... (they, replace)?

Mike: Of course, they .... (replace).
I promised to do it and I did.

Mr Parker: I just can't believe that everything .... (finish, *dt. erledigen*) in just one day …

Mike: You forgot the indicators. They .... (repair), too. And the battery …

Mr Parker: Oh, I think you'd better stop now. What about the bill *(dt. Rechnung)*?

Übung 2

Nach einem Fußballspiel, das Ben und Steve mit ihren Eltern besucht haben, merkt Steve, dass seine Kamera gestohlen wurde. Auf der Polizeistation herrscht gerade großer Andrang. Bilde Passivsätze, falls es sinnvoll ist, mit *by-agent*.

1. Ben: Someone has stolen my camera.

   My camera ....

2. A girl: Two boys have damaged (damage, *dt. beschädigen*) my bike.

   ....

3. Mr Thompson: Someone has smashed three windows of my house.

   Three windows of my house ....

4. Liza Hardy: Someone has searched through my wardrobe. (search through, *dt. durchsuchen*).

   ....

Übung 3

Als die Parkers nach Hause kommen, ist die ganze Wohnung blitzblank. War Mr X da? – Vervollständige den Dialog mit Verbformen im Present Perfect Passive.

Mrs Parker: Fred, Ben, Steve! Quick! Come here! Look at this … Am I dreaming? Everything's spick and span *(dt. blitzblank)*.

The floor .... (clean) and all the carpets .... (vacuum, *dt. staubsaugen*).

Ben *(from upstairs)*: Hey, what's this? My room .... (tidy up). – What about yours, Steve?

Steve: Mine .... (clean), too.

Mr Parker: Oh, look at this … The shopping .... (already, do) and the table .... (lay) (lay the table, *dt. den Tisch decken*).

Sarah: Hi, everybody. Julie and I have been playing at being Mr X but you've come back too early. The main course *(dt. Hauptgang bei einem Menü)* .... (not, prepare) yet and the dishes .... (not, wash).

Mrs Parker: Never mind, this is a wonderful surprise. Thanks a lot!

4. Past Perfect Simple

Verwendung / Signalwörter → *siehe Aktivform, Kap. 15, S. 34*

Bildung:

bejahter Satz *had* + *been* + 3. Form	→ The Parkers' house had been built before Ben was born.
verneinter Satz *had* + *not* + *been* + 3. Form	→ It hadn't been renovated when they moved in.
Fragesatz (Fragewort +) *had* + Subjekt + *been* + 3. Form	→ Had the house been cleaned by Mr X when the Parkers came back yesterday?

Übung 1

Hier siehst du eine Liste davon, was Sarah und Julie bereits erledigt hatten (und was nicht), als ihre Eltern gestern nach Hause kamen. Bilde Frage- und Antwortsätze im Past Perfect Simple Passive.

	yes	no
1. clean / floor	⊗	○
2. vacuum / carpets	⊗	○
3. tidy up / Ben and Steve's rooms	⊗	○
4. do / shopping	⊗	○
5. prepare / main course	○	⊗
6. lay / table	⊗	○
7. wash / dishes	○	⊗

1. Had the floor .... when Mr and Mrs Parker came back last night? – Yes, it ....

2. .... the carpets ....?
Yes, they ....

3. .... Ben and Steve's rooms ....?
....

4. .... the shopping ....?
....

5. .... the main course ....?
....

6. .... the table ....?

....

7. .... the dishes ....?

....

Übung 2

Sarah berichtet Laura in einem Brief davon, was Steve auf der Polizeistation alles mitbekommen hat. Übersetze den folgenden Auszug ins Deutsche.

… When they left the football stadium, Steve suddenly discovered that his camera had been stolen.
There were lots of other people at the police station.
A girl reported (report, *dt. berichten*) that her bike had been damaged by two boys.
A man called Mr Thompson told the policemen that three windows of his house had been smashed.
And a lady said that her wardrobe had been searched through …

… Als sie das Fußballstadion verließen, entdeckte Steve plötzlich, dass

....

....

....

....

....

....

....

....

....

....

....

....

....

....

....

5. Present Progressive

Verwendung / Signalwörter	→ *siehe Aktivform, Kap. 4, S. 12*
Bildung:	
bejahter Satz *am / are / is* + *being* + 3. Form	→ The bathroom is being cleaned at the moment.
verneinter Satz *am / are / is* + *not* + *being* + 3. Form	→ Steve's computer isn't being used at the moment.
Fragesatz (Fragewort +) *am / are / is* + Subjekt + *being* + 3. Form	→ Are we being followed by the police?

Übung 1

Es ist Samstagmorgen. Was wird gerade von wem erledigt? Forme die Aktiv- in Passivsätze um.

1. Steve is fetching the newspaper (fetch, *dt. holen*).

   The newspaper .... by ....

2. Mrs Parker is making tea and coffee.

   Tea and coffee ....

3. Sarah is putting cereal on the table.

   Cereal .... on the table ....

4. Julie is pouring (pour, *dt. gießen*) milk into a jug *(dt. Krug)*.

   Milk .... into ....

5. Mr Parker is laying the table.

   ....

6. Ben is frying bacon and eggs (fry, *dt. braten*).

   ....

Übung 2

**Am Samstagnachmittag sind die Parkers sehr beschäftigt …
Bilde Frage- und Antwortsätze im Present Progressive Passive.**

Sarah:	clean / Julie's bike	Mr Parker:	cut / grass *(dt. Rasen mähen)*
Steve:	paint / fence *(dt. Zaun)*	Julie:	walk / Mrs Johnson's dog *(dt. mit dem Hund Gassi gehen)*
Ben:	read / magazines		
Mrs Parker:	make / some biscuits		

1. .... Julie's bike .... by Steve?

   No, it .... by Steve, it .... by Sarah.

2. .... the fence .... by Steve?

   Yes, ...

3. .... the magazines .... by Ben?

   ....

4. .... the grass .... by Mr Parker?

   ....

5. .... the biscuits .... by Sarah?

   ....

   ....

6. .... Mrs Johnson's dog .... by Julie?

   ....

Übung 3

Nach vielen Jahren wird nun das ganze Haus der Parkers wieder renoviert. Wo wird gerade was gemacht? Bilde Sätze.

1. a new kitchen / install

   A new kitchen ....

2. dining-room / new wallpaper / put up *(dt. tapezieren)*

   In the dining-room new ....

3. bathroom / a new bathtub *(dt. Badewanne)* and sink *(dt. Waschbecken)* / put in

   ....

4. Julie's room / walls / paint / light blue

   ....

5. Steve's room / a new carpet *(dt. Teppich)* / fit *(dt. verlegen)*

   ....

6. Past Progressive

Verwendung / Signalwörter	→ *siehe Aktivform, Kap. 8, S. 20*
Bildung:	
bejahter Satz *was / were* + *being* + 3. Form	→ Our kitchen was being cleaned at 10 a.m. yesterday.
verneinter Satz *was / were* + *not* + *being* + 3. Form	→ The other rooms weren't being cleaned yesterday morning.
Fragesatz (Fragewort +) *was / were* + Subjekt + *being* + 3. Form	→ Was the burglar being followed by the police all night long?

Übung 1

Als Sarah am Tag nach der großen Renovierung in die Schule kommt, kann sie keine Hausaufgaben vorweisen …
Verwende das Past Progressive Passive.

Sarah: I'm sorry, Mrs Forster, but I couldn't do my homework yesterday. Our whole house ………………………………………… (redecorate, *dt. renovieren*) all day long.

Mrs Forster: I'm sure you could have found somewhere to do it.

Sarah: I really couldn't. A new carpet ………………………………………… (fit) in my room. My twin brother's room needed a new carpet as well. And in my little sister's room the walls ………………………………………… (paint). I wanted to do my homework in my big brother's room, but parquet *(dt. Parkett)* ………………………………………… (lay) there all day long …

Mrs Forster: You could have done your homework in the living-room.

Sarah: I'd have loved to have done it there. But in the living-room a new fireplace ………………………………………… (install).

Mrs Forster: I see … Is there a dining-room in your house?

Sarah: Yes, of course …

Mrs Forster: Why didn't you do your homework there? ………………… a new fireplace ………………………………………… (install) there, too? Or ………………………………………… (walls, paint)?

Sarah: No, the walls .... (not, paint) in the dining-room, but new wallpaper .... (put up).

Mrs Forster: What about the kitchen?

Sarah: I wanted to do my homework there, but when I walked in, I saw that a new kitchen .... (install). Finally, I even tried the bathroom, but there a new bathtub and sink .... (put in). You see, there was really no chance for me to do my homework …

Mrs Forster: It's okay, Sarah. I see …

Übung 2

Sarah beschreibt Laura, wie es am Tag vorher zu Hause zuging. Verwende die Verbformen aus Übung 1, um den Brief zu vervollständigen.

Liebe Laura,

stell dir vor: Gestern konnte ich keine Hausaufgaben machen, weil das komplette Haus den ganzen Tag lang ....
In meinem Zimmer konnte ich sie nicht erledigen, weil da gerade ein neuer Teppich .... In Julies Zimmer .... die Wände .... In Steves Zimmer war auch ein neuer Teppich fällig. Und in Bens Zimmer .... Parkett ....
Im Wohnzimmer .... ein neuer offener Kamin .... und im Esszimmer ....
In der Küche .... eine neue Kücheneinrichtung .... und selbst im Bad konnte ich keine Hausaufgaben erledigen, weil dort gerade eine neue Badewanne und ein neues Waschbecken .... …

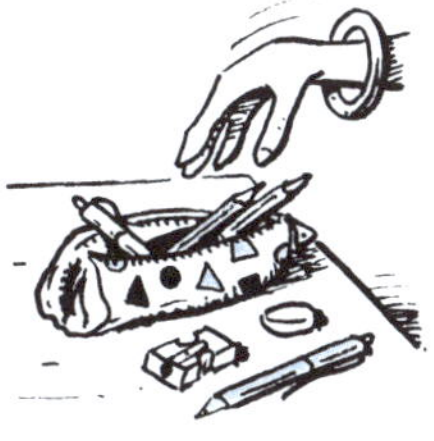

C Abschlusstest

Zeiten-Mix in Aktiv und Passiv

Übung **Hier musst du nun auf alle Zeitformen „gefasst sein", die du in diesem Buch gelernt hast. Achte auf Signalwörter!**

It .... (be) Mr Parker's 44th birthday today. Two hours ago he .... (wake up) by his wife Kelly, who .... (wish) him many happy returns of the day. After he .... (take) a shower, he .... (go) downstairs. Ben, Sarah, Steve and Julie .... (wait) for him in the dining-room. When he .... (come in) they .... (sing) *Happy Birthday*.

"Look, I .... (draw) you a picture, Dad. That's you at the ages of 10, 20, 30 and 40," Julie said. "What a nice idea, Julie." Mr Parker was thrilled.

Sarah and Steve .... (buy) a book for their father. Mr Parker was delighted when he .... (unwrap, *dt. auspacken*) it. "Thanks a lot. I .... (want) this book for ages ..."

"Dad, I .... (not, buy) you anything," Ben said. "These .... (be) just some vouchers *(dt. Gutscheine)* ..." "Well, let me see ... Oh, that's great! I .... (nicht müssen) mow the lawn any more this year. And this one .... (say) that the newspaper will be fetched by you every morning. Thank you very much!"

It's early in the afternoon now.

Mr Parker: "........................ (not, be) that strange? None of my friends or relatives .... (phone) me so far. Kelly, ... (you, think) that they .... (forget) my birthday?"

Mrs Parker: .... (worry, not), Fred.

Steve: Mum, Dad ... We .... (leave) now ...

Mr Parker: Where .... (you, go)?

Steve: Daddy, I always .... (play) tennis on Saturdays at 3 p.m. And Ben, Julie and Sarah .... (have got) some very important things to do. I've got to go now … Bye …

Mr Parker: That's a pity! All the children .... (go). I thought we could have a nice little birthday party …

Mrs Parker: Fred, you .... (not, want) a birthday party!

A few hours later …

Mrs Parker: Fred, you .... (not, have) a present from me yet. But it .... (not, be) here. You have to come with me …

Mr and Mrs Parker .... (drive) to a little hut in a forest nearby …

"Come in, here's my present to you," Mrs Parker says. "Here, in this dark hut?" Mr Parker asks. Suddenly the lights .... (turn on). Mr Parker .... (can, believe, not) his eyes: all his friends and relatives .... (stand) there.

Mr Parker: A surprise party! I .... (not, believe) it! Now I .... (know) why nobody .... (call) me … The room .... (look) great. When .... (decorate) it so beautifully?

Sarah: This afternoon, of course.

Mrs Parker: Sit down, Fred. Look, dinner .... (serve) now. The meal .... (prepare) by a party service.

Julie: .... (you, like) our surprise party, Daddy?

Mr Parker: It's the most wonderful birthday I .... (ever, have). Thank you all so much!

D Zeitenüberblick

Übung

Hier kannst du dir *(last but not least!)* einen Überblick anlegen zu allen Zeitformen, die in diesem Buch behandelt wurden. Setze jeweils die richtige Form des Verbs *to clean* ein.

Aktiv	**Simple Form**	**Progressive Form**
Present Tense	I .... my room every week. Julie .... her room once a month.	I .... my room now. You .... your room right now. Steve .... his room at the moment.
Past Tense	Mrs Parker .... the whole house yesterday.	I .... my room yesterday at 6 p.m. Steve and Sarah .... their rooms yesterday between 1 p.m. and 2 p.m.
Present Perfect	I .... just .... my room. Ben .... already .... his room.	I .... my room since 3 p.m. Julie .... her room for half an hour now.
Past Perfect	After he .... his room, Ben went swimming.	After she .... her room for an hour, Julie went to bed.

Passiv	Simple Form	Progressive Form
Present Tense	The kitchen .... daily. The bedrooms .... every week.	The kitchen .... right now. The bedrooms .... at the moment.
Past Tense	Julie's room .... last week. Ben and Steve's rooms .... yesterday.	The living-room .... at 4 p.m. yesterday. Ben and Steve's rooms .... yesterday between 1 p.m. and 2 p.m.
Present Perfect	Sarah's room .... just .... The hall and the living-room .... already	Keine Progressive Form!!!
Past Perfect	After the rooms ...., the Parkers went out.	Keine Progressive Form!!!

Nach dem Heraustrennen bitte hier klammern

mentor Übungsbuch

Englisch

7./8. Klasse

Die Zeiten: Bildung und Verwendung

Verena Rotter

Lösungsteil

(an der Perforation heraustrennen)

mentor
Eine Klasse besser.

6 7 A Aktiv
1. Simple Present: Bejahte Sätze

Übung 1

The Parkers live in Bristol.
Mr Parker works as a computer programmer in a big company.
The Parkers have four children: Ben, Steve, Sarah and Julie.
Ben, who is 17, attends the last year of grammar school.
He wants to go to university afterwards.
His girl-friend Emma lives in Bristol, too. She works in a hospital as a nurse.
Sarah and Steve are twins. They are 13 years old and attend a big comprehensive school. Julie, who is eight, loves going to her elementary school.

Übung 2

Sarah and Steve get up at 7.30 on weekdays.
Sarah often spends half an hour in the bathroom and then hurries to catch the bus.
She says, "I really love school but my brother hates it. He only likes P.E.
Steve plays tennis in the school team and he never misses a match on TV.
My favourite teacher is Mr Harrison. He comes from Newcastle and teaches geography."

Übung 3

1. Ben likes technology but he hates French.
2. Steve and Sarah like P.E. but they hate science.
3. Julie likes art but she hates history.
4. I like (maths / English ...) but I hate (geography / biology ...).
   Hier fügst du dein persönliches Lieblingsfach ein bzw. das, was du überhaupt nicht magst. Falls du Fächer gewählt hast, die in diesem Buch nicht vorkommen, kannst du in einem Lexikon die richtige Schreibweise kontrollieren.

Übung 4

1. Ben gets up at 7 o'clock every morning.
2. He sometimes uses his motorbike to get to school. / Sometimes he uses ...
3. Ben often watches films on TV in the evening.

Häufigkeitsadverbien wie z. B. always, often, sometimes *und* never *stehen a) vor dem Vollverb, b) nach einer Form von* to be *oder c) nach dem 1. Hilfsverb.* Sometimes *kann auch am Satzanfang stehen.*

Da im Übungsteil nicht weiter auf die Sonderformen der Verben to be *und* to have *im* Simple Present *eingegangen wurde, hier nochmals eine kleine Wiederholung:*

to be	*I am*	***to have***	*I have*
	you are		*you have*
	he / she / it is		*he / she / it has*
	we are		*we have*
	you are		*you have*
	they are		*they have*

2. Simple Present: Verneinte Sätze

8 9

Im Englischen kannst du z. B. bei Verneinungen entweder die Kurzform (z. B. don't) *oder die Langform* (do not) *wählen. Beides ist richtig.*
Der besseren Übersichtlichkeit halber findest du in der Regel im Folgenden nur eine Form.
Im mündlichen Sprachgebrauch sind Kurzformen generell üblicher.

Übung 1

Sarah is good at school but she isn't the best pupil in her class. She speaks German fairly well but she can't / cannot speak Italian.
Her parents are happy when she gets a good mark but they aren't angry with her when she gets a bad one. Her twin brother Steve often asks her: "Do you know how to solve this maths problem?" Mostly, Sarah's answer is, "No, I haven't got a clue."
Sarah's favourite subject is geography but she isn't good at biology and she can't stand physics. She says "I really like school but I'm not a swot."

Übung 2

Sarah continues: "I like German but I don't like our German teacher, Mr March. He doesn't explain anything at all and he doesn't help us when we've got a problem. Vicky and I often don't understand a single word because he speaks so fast. He gives us loads of homework but he doesn't correct it. That's a shame, isn't it?
Sometimes I think that he doesn't like teaching at all."

Übung 3

1. Sarah and Steve Parker must get up at 7.30 in the morning on weekdays but they may stay in bed as long as they like on Saturdays and Sundays.
2. Mrs Parker always tells them to hurry in the morning because they mustn't miss their bus.
   If Steve and Sarah miss the bus, they must go to school by bike. Last week, Sarah's bike had a puncture. Her mother said, "You may use mine instead."
3. Mr Holden, their physics teacher, is very strict. He once said, "You mustn't forget to do your homework, otherwise you must stay in school all night long." Sarah was really shocked but a friend told her: "You needn't be afraid of him. He was only joking."

Übung 4

1. In England school doesn't begin at eight o'clock.
2. German pupils haven't got assembly in the morning.
3. In England school doesn't finish at 1 p.m.
4. Very often German pupils can't have lunch at school.

Hast du alle Verben richtig verneint? Nicht vergessen:
a) Vollverben werden im Simple Present *mithilfe von* do / does *verneint.*
b) Hilfsverben müssen nicht umschrieben werden.

10 | 11

3. Simple Present: Fragesätze

Bei der Bildung von Fragesätzen im Simple Present *musst du beachten:*
a) Vollverben werden (abgesehen von Subjektfragen) mit do / does *umschrieben*
b) Hilfsverben müssen nicht umschrieben werden

Übung 1

1. Can Sarah help Julie with her maths homework?
2. Does she help her every day?
3. Do Sarah and Vicky play tennis in the school team?
4. Are they good tennis players?
5. Is Ben good at writing essays?
6. Does he write an essay every week?

Übung 2

1. When does Julie get up?
2. Who makes breakfast for her?
   Subjektfrage → keine Umschreibung.
3. What can Julie use to get to school?
   Hier ist bereits ein Hilfsverb (can) *vorhanden → keine Umschreibung.*
4. How much does Julie's schoolbag weigh?
5. Which subject / What does Julie like?
   Hier wird nach dem Objekt gefragt, also ist eine Umschreibung nötig.

Übung 3

1. Do you like school?
2. Which subjects do you teach?
3. Where do you live?
4. When do you have to get up on schooldays?
   Have to *(Ersatzverb von* must*) muss in der Frage umschrieben werden.*
5. Can you walk to school?
6. Do you have a car?
   Have *ist hier ein Vollverb → Umschreibung.*
   Falls du Have you got a car? *geschrieben hast, ist das auch richtig.*
7. Are you married?
8. Does your wife work?
   Hast du daran gedacht, dass your wife *3. Pers. Sing. ist? → Umschreibung mit* does.
9. Have you got any children?
   Have *ist hier ein Hilfsverb → keine Umschreibung.*
10. How old are you?
11. Do you play tennis?

4. Present Progressive

12 : 13

Übung 1

getting *(Konsonantenverdopplung)*
carrying
taking *(stummes* -e *entfällt)*
stopping *(Konsonantenverdopplung)*
going
leaving *(stummes* -e *entfällt)*
flying
running *(Konsonantenverdopplung)*

Übung 2

1. Julie is visiting her friend Jackie.
2. Ben and Emma are watching a video.
3. Mr Parker is putting up a new fence.
4. Steve and his friend Eric are surfing the Net.
5. Mrs Parker is baking a cake.
6. Sarah is helping her mother.

Übung 3

Auch zu den Formen von to be *gibt es, wie du sicher weißt, Kurzformen. Diese kommen vor allem (wie z. B. hier) in der gesprochenen Sprache vor. Selbstverständlich sind auch hierbei die vollen Formen richtig.*

Just as Mrs Parker is putting the cake into the oven the phone rings. "Sarah, would you please answer the phone?" she asks. Sarah lifts the receiver. "Who's calling?" Mrs Parker wants to know. "It's Auntie Heather." "Tell her to hang on … I'm coming."

Mrs Parker: Hello, Heather. How are you? … What are you doing?
Heather: Jim and I are sitting in the garden. We are just having a nice cup of tea.
Just *steht nach der Form von* to be*!*
And what's going on at your place, Kelly?
Mrs Parker: Well, my husband is working in the garden.
Heather: Is he cutting the grass again?
Mrs Parker: No, Fred is putting up a new fence today.
Heather: And the kids? What are they doing?
Mrs Parker: Well, Julie is visiting Jackie. Ben and Emma are lying (-ie *wird* zu -y-!) in front of the telly, Steve is sitting in front of the computer and Sarah isn't doing anything special at the moment. She is just listening to what I'm telling you now."

Merke:
Die „Sonderformen in der Schreibweise" gelten natürlich nicht nur für das Present Progressive, *sondern auch für alle anderen Verlaufsformen.*

14 | 15

5. Simple Present und Present Progressive im Vergleich

Signalwörter sind im Folgenden unterstrichen!

Übung 1

1. Ben usually takes a shower in the morning.
   Usually *muss vor dem Vollverb stehen!*
2. Steve often plays tennis in the afternoon.
   But he isn't playing tennis at the moment. He is reading.
   At the moment *bezieht sich auch noch auf den nachfolgenden Satz.*
3. What is Mrs Parker doing right now? – She is putting up the curtains.
   Auch hier wird im zweiten Satz von einer momentanen Tätigkeit gesprochen.
4. Mr Parker works in a computer firm. That's his job.
   Der Nachsatz That's his job. *unterstreicht, dass es hier um Mr Parkers berufliche, also regelmäßige Tätigkeit geht* → Simple Form.
   Hast du an das -s gedacht?
   At the moment he is working in the garden.
5. Julie doesn't tidy up her room very often. She hates doing it.
   Nicht vergessen: Verneinte Vollverben müssen mit to do *umschrieben werden!*

Übung 2

Dear Vicky,
I'm writing this letter in a café in Inverness.
Mum, Julie and I are sitting here and we are having a nice cup of tea.
Hier beschreibt Sarah, wo sie gerade ist und was sie gerade tut → Progressive Form.
The weather is fine today.
We get up late every morning. Dad gets up first and makes breakfast for us.
After breakfast we usually go walking. Ben sometimes uses his mountain bike to get up the hills. The countryside is beautiful and I simply love these Highland cattle – you know, the ones with the long hair.
Hast du daran gedacht, dass Zustandsverben immer in der Simple Form *stehen?*
Mum and Julie are leaving now. Gotta go!
See you soon. Love, Sarah

Übung 3

Julie: Dad, what do you know about Nessie?
Mr Parker: Ask Steve. He is (just) reading a book about Nessie.
Signalwort: gerade → Progressive Form.
Julie: Steve, do you think / believe that Nessie really lives here?
Signalwort: glauben → *Zustandsverb.*
Steve: I don't know. Look! Something is moving over there …
Signalwort: Schau! (→ *Steve macht Julie darauf aufmerksam, was gerade passiert.*)
Hast du bei Frage / Verneinung in der Simple Form *an die Umschreibung mit* to do *gedacht?*

6. Simple Past: Bejahte Sätze

16 17

Übung 1

bought
drove
travelled *(BE)* / traveled *(AE)**
sent
wrote
returned
said
told

* *BE = British English / AE = American English*

Übung 2

Ben: Hi, Emma! I'm back.
Emma: Hello, dear! I missed you. Did you enjoy your holiday?
Ben: Of course I did. The weather was nice and we had a lot of fun – well, most of the time …
Actually, I broke my right arm three days ago.
Emma: Oh dear! What happened?
Ben: I simply fell off my bike when I was going down a bumpy road.
My father took me to hospital.
The doctors there put my arm in plaster.

Übung 3

Sarah's diary:
We left Glasgow at 8 a.m. Dad drove all the way to Perth. In the afternoon we arrived at our holiday flat. It looked awful. Mum and I had to clean the floor first. Julie and Steve washed the dirty dishes and Dad and Ben went shopping, because we needed some food for dinner. After dinner we watched a funny film on TV.

Vicky's diary:
I slept till 10 o'clock this morning. After breakfast I helped Mum with the shopping.
In the afternoon it got really hot, so Karen and I decided to go swimming.
Zur Erinnerung: to get *kann* werden *und* bekommen *heißen!*
Today we swam a mile in less than an hour. Dad was really proud of me when he heard about it. Karen and I were extremely tired afterwards, so we spent the rest of the day in the garden lying lazily in the sun …

Sicher hast du gemerkt, dass man für die Verbformen im Simple Past *fit in den unregelmäßigen Verben sein muss. Wie wär's mit einer kleinen Wiederholung?*

18 | 19

7. Simple Past: Verneinte Sätze und Fragesätze

Übung 1

1. The Parkers were *in Wales* last week.
   No, they weren't in Wales. They were in Scotland.
2. The Parkers went *by train*.
   No, they didn't go by train. They went by car.
3. The Parkers stayed *in a hotel* in Perth.
   No, they didn't stay in a hotel. They stayed in a holiday flat.
4. Sarah saw lots of *kangaroos* in Scotland.
   No, she didn't see kangaroos. She saw Highland cattle.
5. Ben broke his *leg* in Scotland.
   No, Ben didn't break his leg. He broke his arm.
6. Julie was *happy* when they left Scotland.
   No, she wasn't happy. She was sad.

Übung 2

1. Was the weather nice in Scotland?
2. Where did you stay?
3. Did you see Nessie?
4. Who took Ben to hospital?
   Subjektfrage → keine Umschreibung.
5. When did you return?

Übung 3

Hi, Sarah,
How was your holiday?
Did you like Scotland?
Did you see *Higland cattle*?
We didn't go on holiday because my parents didn't have enough money.
Have *ist hier ein Vollverb, also muss es in der Verneinung mit* did *umschrieben werden.*
But I wasn't sad, because the weather was nice here, too.
Please, write to me soon. Laura

8. Past Progressive

20 | 21

Übung 1

1. Mr Parker was having a meeting with colleagues.
   Have *ist hier ein Tätigkeitsverb, also kann es in der* Progressive Form *stehen.*
2. Mrs Parker was buying some clothes.
3. Steve and Eric were playing tennis.
4. Ben was repairing his motorbike.
5. Julie was doing her homework.
6. Sarah and Vicky were sitting in front of the telly.

Übung 2

While Mr Parker was scrubbing the floor,
Hast du hier an die Konsonantenverdopplung gedacht?
Mrs Parker was vacuuming.
Sarah and Steve were taking down the curtains, while Julie was wiping out the cupboards.
Hier entfällt das stumme -e!
Mrs Parker's sister Heather was helping, too. She was cleaning the windows.
Ben was the only one who wasn't working. He was lying on the sofa the whole time, because he still had his arm in plaster.
Hier musst du wieder -ie *in* -y- *umwandeln!*

Übung 3

Inspector:	Well, Mr Hunter, what were you doing yesterday at 4 p.m.?
Mr Hunter:	I was working. *Die Antwort bezieht sich auf die Zeitangabe* (gestern um 16 Uhr). *Also steht auch hier die Verlaufsform.*
Inspector:	Where were you working?
Mr Hunter:	I was just selling a brand-new car in my shop.
Inspector:	And you, Mr Thomas? What were you doing at the time the robbery took place?
Mr Thomas:	Of course I wasn't robbing the bank. My wife and I were walking our dog Jessie between 3.30 and 4 o'clock. Then we met some friends and we were having tea with them till 5 p.m.
Inspector:	What about you, Mrs Oldham? What were you doing yesterday at 4 p.m.?
Mrs Oldham:	Well, at 4 p.m. I was chatting to my neighbour, Mrs Donovan. *Hast du an die Konsonantenverdopplung gedacht?* We were sitting in her living-room. She can testify to this, of course. You know, we were talking about …
Inspector:	Thank you, Mrs Oldham, that's enough for the moment …

22 23 9. Simple Past und Past Progressive im Vergleich

Übung 1

In diesem Bericht schildert Julie mehrere, kurz aufeinander folgende Ereignisse. Daher ist hier das Simple Past *zu verwenden.*

"I don't know how it happened. I suddenly stumbled and fell down. My left knee bled. It really hurt but I didn't cry.
Jackie, who saw me lying on the ground, came to me at once. Then she sent Daniel to look for a teacher. Mrs Bell, who was there within two minutes, had a first-aid kit with her. First she put a bandage on my knee. Then she went to our maths teacher, Mr Collins, and told him that I needed some rest.
That's why I didn't have to write the maths test today … Wasn't I lucky?"

Hast du 's noch gewusst? Have to *ist das Ersatzverb zu* must.
Da have *in diesem Fall ein Vollverb ist, muss es in der Verneinung mit* did *umschrieben werden.*

Übung 2

In dieser Übung geht es um mehrere Handlungen in der Vergangenheit, die gleichzeitig stattfanden. Deshalb stehen die Verbformen im Past Progressive.

1. While Steve and Eric were buying some soft drinks, Tom was getting some crackers.
2. While Justin was looking for a place for the camp fire, David was collecting some wood.
3. While everybody else was sunbathing, Joe and Paul were building a big sandcastle.

Übung 3

Der Satz „Was passierte plötzlich?" weist darauf hin, dass eine Handlung in der Vergangenheit von einer anderen unterbrochen wurde.
In so einem Fall steht die erste Handlung im Past Progressive *und die zweite im* Simple Past.
Das Signalwort while *zeigt an, welche Handlung bereits im Verlauf war.*

1. While Steve was carrying ten cans of lemonade, a ball hit his head and he dropped the cans.
   Hit *und* dropped *sind zwei Handlungen, die gleich hintereinander passierten, also müssen beide im* Simple Past *stehen.*
   Hast du bei drop *an die Konsonantenverdopplung gedacht?*
2. A mosquito bit Dave while he was collecting wood for the camp fire.
3. While Joe and Paul were building the sandcastle, a big wave suddenly came and washed it away.
   Die Ereignisse came *und* washed it away *passierten unmittelbar hintereinander, also muss hier beide Male die* Simple Form *stehen.*

10. Present Perfect Simple

24 25

Übung 1

1. Mr and Mrs Parker have known each other since 1980.
2. The Parkers have lived in their house for more than 17 years now.
3. Steve hasn't had a haircut for a long time.
4. Sarah hasn't seen her grandparents since last Christmas.
5. Julie hasn't tidied up her room for three weeks.

Nicht vergessen: In Verbindung mit seit … *verwendet man im Deutschen nicht das Perfekt, sondern das Präsens (die Gegenwart).*
Satz 1 heißt übersetzt: Mr und Mrs Parker kennen sich seit 1980.

Übung 2

Auch im Present Perfect *kann das Hilfsverb in einer Kurzform auftreten:*
have → 've / has → 's

Mrs Parker: Sarah, have you done the washing up?
Sarah: It's Steve's turn today. But as far as I know, he hasn't washed the dishes yet.
Mrs Parker: Steve, why haven't you done the washing up?
Steve: I'm sorry. I forgot. But look, I've cleared the table and I've put most of the stuff into the dishwasher. I'll do the washing up later …
Mrs Parker: No, you won't. You've got to do it now. – Where is Julie? Juuuuuuuuliiiieeee!!!! Have you tidied up your room yet? It looked awful this morning! … *(no answer)*
Sarah: Perhaps she's already left.
But she *has* tidied up her room.
Die volle Form (has) *erscheint hier sinnvoller, da Sarah betont, dass Julie ihr Zimmer bereits aufgeräumt gemacht hat.*
I've just seen it. It looks great now …
Just *muss hier zwischen Hilfsverb und Vollverb stehen.*

Übung 3

Im schriftlichen Sprachgebrauch sind Kurzformen vor allem bei informellen Briefen üblich.

Dear Sarah,
I haven't heard from you for three weeks. Are you still alive? I can't wait to hear about your holiday in Scotland. Unfortunately, I've never been to Scotland.
Wales must be great, too. Have you ever been there?
Never *und* ever *stehen vor dem Vollverb!*
Although we haven't been away on holiday this year, I didn't get bored.
I've just taken up riding.
I've had two lessons so far. Have you ever ridden a horse?
I think it's wonderful … Write soon. Love, Laura

Bei regelmäßigen Verben wird die 3. Form ebenso wie die 2. Form (Grundform + -ed) gebildet. Die „Sonderformen in der Schreibweise", wie sie für die 2. Form gelten (→ Kap. 6, S. 16), sind daher auch auf die 3. Form anzuwenden.

26 27

11. Present Perfect Progressive

Übung 1

1. Mr and Mrs Parker have been gardening all day.
2. Steve has been playing games on his computer.
3. Julie has been walking her friend's dog since 7 a.m.
4. Ben has been lying on his bed for three hours.
   Nicht vergessen: -ie *wird in der* Progressive Form *zu* -y-*!*
5. Sarah has been sitting on a bench in the garden all day.
   She and Vicky have been talking to each other on the phone since 11 a.m.

Übung 2

Mrs Parker: Hello Steve, how was your day?
Steve: I'm exhausted, Mum. I've been playing basketball since 2 p.m. I'm really shattered now …
Mrs Parker: And what about you, Sarah? What have you been doing all afternoon?
Sarah: Vicky and I have been chatting on the Net with two German students, Lars and Nick. What about your day, Mum? Have you been working hard today?
Mrs Parker: Well, I've been washing clothes all day.
Sarah: What about Dad and Ben?
Mrs Parker: Ben has been writing letters since 1 p.m. and Dad has been trying to repair the toaster …

Übung 3

English	German
Sarah: How long have you and Nick been chatting on the Net today?	Wie lange chattet ihr / chatten du und Nick heute schon im Internet?
We've been chatting for two hours. *In Verbindung mit* seit *musst du hier statt der Gegenwart im Deutschen das* Present Perfect *verwenden. Da* seit zwei Stunden *ein Zeitraum ist, musst du* for *verwenden.*	Lars: Wir chatten seit zwei Stunden.
Sarah: How long have you and Nick been learning English?	Wie lange lernt ihr / lernen du und Nick schon Englisch? / Seit wann …
We've been learning English for eight years.	Lars: Wir lernen seit acht Jahren Englisch.
Nick has been studying English for two years.	Nick studiert Englisch seit zwei Jahren.
Zeiträume → for.	

12. Present Perfect Simple und Present Perfect Progressive im Vergleich

28 29

Übung 1

1. Steve has had his computer for three years.
   Have *in der Bedeutung* besitzen *ist ein Zustandsverb* → Simple Form.
2. He has been playing computer games for 30 minutes now.
   Spielen *ist eine Tätigkeit* → Progressive Form.
3. Ben and Emma have been together for a long time. *(Zustand)*
4. Vicky and Sarah have been delivering newspapers all day. *(Tätigkeit)*
5. Julie has been drawing a picture since 1 p.m. *(Tätigkeit)*
6. She has loved art ever since her first lesson in it. *(Zustand)*

Übung 2

Mrs Parker: Hello, Heather, what have you been doing all day?
Betonung der Dauer (den ganzen Tag lang) → Progressive Form.

Heather: I've been gardening since 10 a.m.
Since + *Tätigkeitsverb* → Progressive Form.
I've been planting new trees and bushes.
Genauere Erläuterung der Tätigkeit → Progressive Form.

Mrs Parker: That sounds great. I haven't planted trees for years.
How many have you planted so far?
In diesen beiden Sätzen steht das Ergebnis (keine *bzw.* wie viele?) *im Vordergrund* → Simple Form.

Heather: About twenty. And what have you been doing on such a beautiful day?
Hier ist wieder die Dauer betont → Progressive Form.

Mrs Parker: Well, I've been baking cakes all day for Julie's birthday party.
Betonung der Dauer → Progressive Form.
We haven't had a big party for a long time …

Übung 3

1. Mr Parker and his brother Mike have been catching fish all day.
2. Ben hasn't read a single book today.
   Die Gegenfrage wäre hier How many books …?" → *Die Betonung liegt also auf dem Ergebnis.*
3. Vicky and Sarah have known each other for years.
   Zwar wird hier die Dauer betont (seit vielen Jahren),
   know *ist jedoch ein Zustandsverb* → Simple Form.
4. Mr Collins has been correcting the maths tests all afternoon.
5. Has Laura ever been to Scotland?

Bei der Entscheidung Present Perfect Simple / Present Perfect Progressive *musst du zweierlei überprüfen:*
a) Handelt es sich um ein Tätigkeits- oder um ein Zustandsverb?
b) Wird die Dauer oder das Ergebnis betont?
Das Present Perfect Progressive *steht nur dann, wenn es sich*
1. um eine Tätigkeit handelt und
2. die Dauer betont wird.

30 31

13. Past Tense und Present Perfect im Vergleich

Übung 1

Simple Past	Present Perfect Simple
he worked	he has worked
I didn't go	I haven't gone
they arrived	they have arrived
you didn't see	you haven't seen
she didn't talk	she hasn't talked

Übung 2

1. Sarah has received three letters this month.
2. Two days ago she got a very long letter from Laura.
3. Steve and Sarah have written four tests this week.
4. The maths test last Tuesday was the most difficult one.
6. Mr Parker married his wife in 1981.
5. They have been married for a long time now.

Übung 3

Bei dieser Übung durftest du dich nicht von der Verwendung des Perfekts im Deutschen in die Irre führen lassen!
Weist ein Signalwort auf einen abgeschlossenen Zeitpunkt hin, musst du im Englischen das Past Tense *verwenden, ganz gleich, ob im deutschen Satz das Imperfekt oder das Perfekt steht.*

Vicky: Hi, Sarah! What did you do last night / yesterday evening?
Last night *ist gebräuchlicher.*

Sarah: I went to Peter's party. – Why didn't you come?
Diese Sätze beziehen sich auch auf gestern Abend → Past Tense.

Vicky: Peter didn't invite me. – Was it good?
Hier ist auch ohne Signalwort klar:
Der Zeitpunkt der Einladung ist vorbei → Past Tense.

Sarah: It was great. I met Sam again.
Die Party (und damit das Treffen) ist vorbei → Past Tense.
We've known each other for two weeks.
Nicht vergessen: Das deutsche seit … *muss im Englischen mit dem* Present Perfect *wiedergegeben werden;* know = *Zustandsverb* → Simple Form.
Have you ever met Sam?
Sehen *musst du hier mit* meet *übersetzen.*

Vicky: No, I've never seen him.

14. Past Tense und Present Perfect: Simple und Progressive Forms

32 33

Übung 1

Simple Past
I didn't go
we weren't
it started
I noticed
they carried

Present Perfect Simple
I have swum
you haven't seen
he has been
have you started
we have begun

Past Progressive
he was singing
we were celebrating
they were jumping
what were you doing
I was sitting

Present Perfect Progressive
she hasn't been walking
they have been playing
she has been teasing
we haven't been talking
have you been lying

Übung 2

Heather: Hello, darling, many happy returns of the day!
What have you been doing all day?
Der Geburtstag ist noch nicht vorbei → Present Perfect.
Betonung der Dauer (den ganzen Tag lang) → Progressive Form.

Julie: Well, I didn't sleep late this morning. I got up quite early.
Der Morgen und das Aufstehen sind vorbei → Past Tense.
When I came downstairs, Mum and Dad were still wrapping some of my birthday presents.

Heather: What did you get for your birthday, then?

Julie: I got a brand-new *Glamour Barbie* and a fantastic cake.
Steve and Sarah gave me some coloured pencils and I received a colouring book from Ben.
Julie hat die Geschenke bereits bekommen → Past Tense.

Heather: Did you have a birthday party in the afternoon?
Der Nachmittag ist vorbei → Past Tense.

Julie: Well, it isn't over yet. We have been celebrating for five hours now.
Die Party ist noch nicht vorbei → Present Perfect.
Hier ist die Dauer betont → Progressive Form.
We have played lots of different games and we have already eaten up four cakes …
Hier wäre die Gegenfrage How many? → *Ergebnis ist betont* → Simple Form.
Nicht vergessen: already *steht zwischen dem Hilfs- und dem Vollverb.*

34 35 15. Past Perfect Simple und Progressive

Übung 1

1. + f) After Steve had been sunbathing for hours, his skin turned red.
2. + d) Julie's room had looked a mess before she cleaned it.
3. + a) After she had been writing for three hours, Sarah's right hand started to hurt.
4. + e) Julie began to unwrap her presents after she had thanked everybody.
5. + c) After the children had been playing for five hours, they got tired.
6. + b) Jackie felt sick after she had eaten four pieces of cake.

Übung 2

Simple Form	**Progressive Form**
they had sat	you had been sitting
we hadn't watched	she hadn't been watching
I hadn't drunk	it hadn't been drinking
had you called?	had he been calling?

Übung 3

1. After they had been talking for hours, Vicky and Sarah finally fell asleep.
   Tätigkeit → Progressive Form.
2. Before they got married, Mr and Mrs Parker had known each other for a long time.
   Zustand → Simple Form.
3. After Ben had had the plaster on his arm for three weeks, the doctors removed it.
   Zustand
4. After she had been washing dirty clothes all day, Mrs Parker got sick of all the housework.
   Tätigkeit

Übung 4

1. After Mr Parker had got up, he took a shower.
2. After he had had breakfast, he drove to work.
3. After he had been working for eight hours, he called it a day.
   Hier ist die Dauer (acht Stunden lang) *betont* → Progressive Form.

> *Auch im* Past Perfect *existiert eine Kurzform:*
> *Beispiel:* he had watched → he'd watched ('d + 3. Form)
> *Achtung!*
> *Diese Form ist nicht mit dem* Conditional I *(Kurzform* he'd watch *für* he would watch) *zu verwechseln.*
> *Das* Conditional I *wird mit* 'd (für would) + Grundform *gebildet!*

16. Past Tense und Past Perfect im Vergleich

36 37

Übung 1

1. After she had woken up the kids, she prepared breakfast.
2. After she had cleared the table, she washed the dishes.
3. After she had cleaned the windows, she tidied up the rooms.
   Hast du daran gedacht, das -y- von tidy *in -ie- umzuwandeln?*
4. After she had gone shopping, she made dinner.
5. After she had ironed fifteen shirts, she went to bed.

Übung 2

Aus der Tabelle kannst du entnehmen, welche Handlung zuerst passierte.
Die 1. Handlung muss im Past Perfect *stehen.*
Die 2. Handlung steht im Past Tense.

1. After Ben had done his homework, he went to the cinema.
2. Before Julie and Jackie visited a friend, they had gone swimming.
3. Before Sarah called Vicky, she had read a comic.
4. After Steve had played tennis, he took a shower.

> *Nicht vergessen:*
> after + Past Perfect
> before + Past Tense, *das* Past Perfect *steht dann im anderen Satzteil*

Übung 3

Dear Sarah,
Yesterday was an awful day.
I wanted to have breakfast, but my brother had already eaten up my cornflakes.
Zuerst aß Lauras Bruder die Cornflakes auf, → 1st action → Past Perfect,
dann wollte sie frühstücken. → 2nd action → Simple Past.
When I got / came to the bus-stop, the bus had already left.
Erst ist der Bus abgefahren, → Past Perfect,
dann kam Laura zur Bushaltestelle. → Simple Past.
Hast du die Stellung von already *beachtet?*
After I had been walking for 45 minutes, I finally arrived at school.
Da hier die Dauer betont ist und es sich bei walk *um ein Tätigkeitsverb handelt, steht hier das* Past Perfect Progressive.
But the first lesson had already begun …
Zuerst fing die Stunde an, → Past Perfect,
dann kam Laura.

38 | 39

B Passiv
1. Simple Present

Nicht vergessen:
Bei der Umwandlung von einem Aktiv- in einen Passivsatz musst du überprüfen, ob das neue Subjekt (das ehemalige Objekt des Aktivsatzes) in der Einzahl oder in der Mehrzahl steht.
Dann entscheidest du, welche Form von to be *die passende ist.*

Übung 1

Breakfast is prepared by Mr X.
The beds are made by Mr X.
The dishes are washed by Mr X.
The shopping is done by Mr X.
Dinner is served by Mr X.

Übung 2

1. Is breakfast prepared by Mr X?
   No, it isn't prepared by Mr X, but by Mrs Parker.
2. Are the beds made by Mr X?
   No, they aren't made by Mr X, but by Mrs Parker.
3. Are the dishes washed by Mr X?
   No, they aren't washed by Mr X, but by Mrs Parker.
4. Is the shopping done by Mr X?
   No, it isn't done by Mr X, but by Mrs Parker.
5. Is dinner served by Mr X?
   No, it isn't served by Mr X, but by Mrs Parker.

Übung 3

Merke:
Ist das Objekt eines Aktivsatzes ein Personalpronomen, so muss dieses bei der Umwandlung in einen Passivsatz in den Subjektfall gesetzt werden.
Beispiel: Aktivsatz: her *(Objekt)* → Passivsatz: she *(Subjekt)*

1. He is never beaten by Eric.
2. Beautiful pictures are drawn by her.
3. The Parkers' car is usually repaired by Mike.
4. He is often asked for help by Lenny.
5. They are always invited to parties by their classmates.

Hast du alle Häufigkeitsadverbien (always, never *etc.*) *an die richtige Stelle gesetzt?*

2. Simple Past

40 41

Übung 1

1. The oil was checked.
2. A new battery was put in.
3. The brake fluid was refilled.
4. One outside mirror and the windscreen were replaced.
5. The indicators were repaired.
6. A CD player was installed.
7. Finally the whole car was cleaned.

Übung 2

1. America was discovered by Columbus in 1492.
2. The *Mona Lisa* was painted by Leonardo da Vinci.
3. *Neuschwanstein* was built in the 19th century.
4. Goethe was born in 1749.
5. Germany was defeated in World War II.
6. The *Odyssey* was written by Homer.

Übung 3

1. When was Goethe born?
   Falls derjenige, den du gefragt hast, eine falsche Antwort gibt, sagst du:
   No, he wasn't born in … *(falsche Jahreszahl)*, he was born in 1749.
2. When was America discovered?
   No, it wasn't discovered in …, but in 1492.
3. When was *Neuschwanstein* built?
   No, it wasn't built in …, it was built in the 19th century.

Übung 4

Vor ungefähr 1200 Jahren wurde Britannien von den Wikingern überfallen.
Du kannst den Satz im Deutschen auch mit einem Aktivsatz wiedergeben:
… marschierten die Wikinger in Britannien ein.
York wurde von den Wikingern Jorvik genannt.
Die Wikinger landeten auch in Frankreich, wo sie Normannen genannt wurden.
Hier kannst du den englischen Passivsatz mit dem unpersönlichen man *übersetzen:*
… wo man sie Normannen nannte.
(Im Jahre) 1066 wurde King Harold II / König Harald II. von dem Normannen William the Conqueror / Wilhelm dem Eroberer in der Schlacht von Hastings besiegt / geschlagen und getötet.

Tipp: Bei Prüfungen in der Schule solltest du dich vergewissern, ob Eigennamen zu übersetzen sind!

42 : 43

3. Present Perfect Simple

Übung 1

In dieser Übung stehen die Verbformen im Present Perfect, *da es in diesem Dialog darum geht, dass die Reparaturen erledigt wurden und nicht wann.*
Im vorhergehenden Kapitel findest du die Verbformen im Simple Past, *weil die Rede davon ist, was gestern alles gemacht wurde.*

Mr Parker:	Hi, Mike. Is the car okay again?
Mike:	Yes, of course.
Mr. Parker:	Has the oil been checked?
Mike:	Yes, it has been checked.
Mr. Parker:	What about the brake fluid? Has it been refilled?
Mike:	Certainly.
Mr Parker:	And the mirror and the windscreen … – Have they been replaced?
Mike:	Of course, they've / have been replaced. I promised to do it and I did.
Mr Parker:	I just can't believe that everything has been finished in just one day …
Mike:	You forgot the indicators. They've been repaired, too. And the battery …
Mr Parker:	Oh, I think you'd better stop now. What about the bill?

Übung 2

1. Ben:	My camera has been stolen.
2. A girl:	My bike has been damaged by two boys.
	Hier ist der Verursacher bekannt, deshalb wird der by-agent *angefügt.*
3. Mr Thompson:	Three windows of my house have been smashed.
4. Liza Hardy:	My wardrobe has been searched through.

Übung 3

Mrs Parker:	Fred, Ben, Steve! Quick! Come here! Look at this … Am I dreaming? Everything's spick and span. The floor has been cleaned and all the carpets have been vacuumed.
Ben:	Hey, what's this? My room has been tidied up. – What about yours, Steve?
Steve:	Mine has been cleaned, too.
Mr Parker:	Oh, look at this … The shopping has already been done and the table has been laid. *Hast du's noch gewusst?* already *steht, wenn die Verbform mehrere Hilfsverben enthält, nach dem ersten Hilfsverb.*
Sarah:	Hi, everybody. Julie and I have been playing at being Mr X but you've come back too early. The main course hasn't been prepared yet and the dishes haven't been washed.
Mrs Parker:	Never mind, this is a wonderful surprise. Thanks a lot!

4. Past Perfect Simple

44 : 45

Übung 1

1. Had the floor been cleaned when Mr and Mrs Parker came back last night?
   Yes, it had been cleaned.
2. Had the carpets been vacuumed?
   Yes, they had been vacuumed.
3. Had Ben and Steve's rooms been tidied up?
   Yes, they had been tidied up.
4. Had the shopping been done?
   Yes, it had been done.
5. Had the main course been prepared?
   No, it hadn't been prepared.
6. Had the table been laid?
   Yes, it had been laid.
7. Had the dishes been washed?
   No, they hadn't been washed.

Übung 2

… Als sie das Fußballstadion verließen, entdeckte Steve plötzlich, dass seine Kamera / sein Fotoapparat gestohlen worden war.
Auf der Polizeiwache / dem Polizeirevier waren viele andere / eine Menge anderer / ein Haufen anderer Leute.
Ein Mädchen berichtete, dass ihr Fahrrad von zwei Jungen beschädigt worden war.
Ein Mann namens Mr Thompson erzählte den Polizisten, dass drei Fenster von seinem Haus / seines Hauses eingeworfen worden waren.
Und eine Dame sagte / erzählte, dass ihr Kleiderschrank durchsucht worden war.

46 47

5. Present Progressive

Übung 1

1. The newspaper is being fetched by Steve.
2. Tea and coffee are being made by Mrs Parker.
3. Cereal is being put on the table by Sarah.
4. Milk is being poured into a jug by Julie.
5. The table is being laid by Mr Parker.
6. Bacon and eggs are being fried by Ben.

Hast du daran gedacht, das -y- *in* -ie- *umzuwandeln?*

Übung 2

1. Is Julie's bike being cleaned by Steve?
   No, it isn't being cleaned by Steve, it is / it's being cleaned by Sarah.
2. Is the fence being painted by Steve?
   Yes, it is / it's being painted by Steve.
3. Are the magazines being read by Ben?
   Yes, they are being read by Ben.
4. Is the grass being cut by Mr Parker?
   Yes, it is / it's being cut by Mr Parker.
5. Are the biscuits being made by Sarah?
   No, they aren't being made by Sarah, they are being made by Mrs Parker.
6. Is Mrs Johnson's dog being walked by Julie?
   Yes, it is / it's being walked by Julie.

Übung 3

1. A new kitchen is being installed.
2. In the dining-room new wallpaper is being put up.
3. In the bathroom a new bathtub and sink are being put in.
4. In Julie's room the walls are being painted light blue.
5. In Steve's room a new carpet is being fitted.

Die Ortsangaben (z. B. in Julie's room) *können natürlich auch am Satzende stehen.*
Hast du im letzten Satz an die Konsonantenverdopplung gedacht?

6. Past Progressive

48 | 49

Übung 1

Sarah: I'm sorry, Mrs Forster, but I couldn't do my homework yesterday. Our whole house was being redecorated all day long.
Mrs Forster: I'm sure you could have found somewhere to do it …
Sarah: I really couldn't. A new carpet was being fitted in my room. My twin brother's room needed a new carpet as well. And in my little sister's room the walls were being painted. I wanted to do my homework in my big brother's room, but parquet was being laid there all day long …
Mrs Forster: You could have done your homework in the living-room.
Sarah: I'd have loved to have done it there. But in the living-room a new fireplace was being built in.
Mrs Forster: I see … Is there a dining-room in your house?
Sarah: Yes, of course.
Mrs Forster: Why didn't you do your homework there? Was a new fireplace being installed there, too? Or were the walls being painted?
Sarah: No, the walls weren't being painted in the dining-room, but new wallpaper was being put up.
Mrs Forster: What about the kitchen?
Sarah: I wanted to do my homework there, but when I walked in, I saw that a new kitchen was being installed.
Finally, I even tried the bathroom, but there a new bathtub and sink were being put in. You see, there was really no chance for me to do my homework …
Mrs Forster: It's okay, Sarah. I see …

Übung 2

Liebe Laura,
stell dir vor: Gestern konnte ich keine Hausaufgaben machen, weil das komplette Haus den ganzen Tag lang renoviert wurde.
In meinem Zimmer konnte ich sie nicht erledigen, weil da gerade ein neuer Teppich verlegt wurde. In Julies Zimmer wurden gerade die Wände gestrichen.
Wenn du hier das Wort gerade *einfügst, wird deutlicher, dass der Verlauf betont werden soll.*
In Steves Zimmer war auch ein neuer Teppich fällig. Und in Bens Zimmer wurde gerade Parkett verlegt. Im Wohnzimmer wurde gerade ein neuer offener Kamin eingebaut und im Esszimmer wurde gerade tapeziert. In der Küche wurde gerade eine neue Kücheneinrichtung installiert und selbst im Bad konnte ich keine Hausaufgaben erledigen, weil dort gerade eine neue Badewanne und ein neues Waschbecken eingebaut wurden …

Verlaufsformen im Passiv gibt es nur im Present Tense *und im* Past Tense*!*

50 | 51

C Abschlusstest
Zeiten-Mix in Aktiv und Passiv

Übung

It is Mr Parker's 44th birthday today.
Two hours ago he was woken up by his wife Kelly, who wished him many happy returns of the day. After he had taken a shower, he went downstairs.
Ben, Sarah, Steve and Julie were waiting for him in the dining-room.
Die Kinder warteten bereits → Past Progressive.
When he came in they sang *Happy Birthday*.
Dies sind zwei kurz aufeinander folgende Handlungen in der Vergangenheit → Simple Past.
"Look, I've / have drawn you a picture, Dad. (…)
Julie will ihrem Vater sagen, dass sie etwas gemacht hat (und nicht wann) → Present Perfect.
Sarah and Steve had bought a book (…). Mr Parker was delighted when he unwrapped it.
Der Zeitpunkt des Kaufens liegt weiter zurück (→ Past Perfect) *als der Moment, da Mr Parker das Buch auspackt* (→ Past Tense). *Beachte: Konsonantenverdopplung bei* unwrap!
"Thanks a lot. I have wanted this book for ages …"
Zwar wird hier die Dauer (seit Jahren) *betont, wegen des Zustandsverbs aber* → Simple Form.
"Dad, I haven't bought / didn't buy you anything," Ben said.
Hier kannst du Past Tense *oder* Present Perfect *verwenden!*
"These are just some vouchers (…)" – "I needn't / don't have to mow the lawn (…). And this one says (…)"

It's early in the afternoon now. → *Jetzt wird in der Gegenwart erzählt!*

Mr Parker:	"Isn't that strange? None of my friends or relatives have phoned me so far.
	Hier musst du beim Verb die Mehrzahl verwenden!
	Kelly, do you think that they have forgotten my birthday?"
Mrs Parker:	Don't worry, Fred.
Steve:	Mum, Dad … We're / are leaving now …
Mr Parker:	Where are you going? → *Die Frage bezieht sich auch auf den Augenblick.*
Steve:	Daddy, I always play tennis on Saturdays at 3 p.m.
	And Ben, Julie and Sarah have got some very important things to do (…)
Mr Parker:	That's a pity! All the children have gone. (…)
	Die Kinder sind gerade eben gegangen → Present Perfect.
Mrs Parker:	Fred, you didn't want a birthday party!

A few hours later …

Mrs Parker:	Fred, you haven't had a present from me yet.
	But it's not here. You have to come with me …

Mr and Mrs Parker are driving to a little hut in a forest nearby …
Mr und Mrs Parker fahren gerade im Moment → Present Progressive.
(…) Suddenly the lights are turned on. → *Die Lichter werden angemacht!*
Mr Parker can't believe his eyes: all his friends and relatives are standing there …
Hier wird eine momentane Tätigkeit zum Ausdruck gebracht → Present Progressive.

Mr Parker:	I don't believe it! A surprise party! Now I know why nobody called me …
	Trotz now *muss hier die* Simple Form *stehen, da* know *ein Zustandsverb ist.*
	The room looks / is looking great.
	Look *kann in der* Simple *oder* Progressive Form *stehen.*
	When did you decorate it so beautifully?
Sarah:	This afternoon, of course.
Mrs Parker:	Sit down, Fred. Look, dinner is being served now.
	The meal has been prepared / was prepared by a party service.
	Hier kannst du Present Perfect *oder* Simple Past *verwenden.*
Julie:	Do you like our surprise party, Daddy?
Mr Parker:	It's the most wonderful birthday I have ever had. Thank you all so much!

D Zeitenüberblick

52 53

Übung

Aktiv	Simple Form	Progressive Form
Present Tense	I clean my room every week. Julie cleans her room once a month.	I am cleaning my room now. You are cleaning your room right now. Steve is cleaning his room at the moment.
Past Tense	Mrs Parker cleaned the whole house yesterday.	I was cleaning my room yesterday at 6 p.m. Steve and Sarah were cleaning their rooms yesterday between 1 p.m. and 2 p.m.
Present Perfect	I have just cleaned my room. Ben has already cleaned his room.	I have been cleaning my room since 3 p.m. Julie has been cleaning her room for half an hour now.
Past Perfect	After he had cleaned his room, Ben went swimming.	After she had been cleaning her room for an hour, Julie went to bed.

Passiv	Simple Form	Progressive Form
Present Tense	The kitchen is cleaned daily. The bedrooms are cleaned every week.	The kitchen is being cleaned right now. The bedrooms are being cleaned at the moment.
Past Tense	Julie's room was cleaned last week. Ben and Steve's rooms were cleaned yesterday.	The living-room was being cleaned at 4 p.m. yesterday. Ben and Steve's rooms were being cleaned yesterday between 1 p.m. and 2 p.m.
Present Perfect	Sarah's room has just been cleaned. The hall and the study have already been cleaned.	Keine Progressive Form!!!
Past Perfect	After the rooms had been cleaned, the Parkers went out.	Keine Progressive Form!!!

Die Verbform I am being cleaned *gibt es zwar, sie ist im Zeitenüberblick aber nicht aufgeführt, da es das sprechende Zimmer (noch) nicht gibt …*

mentor Übungsbuch

Englisch

7./8. Klasse

If-Sätze, Futurformen

Verena Rotter

Mit praktischem Lösungsteil zum Heraustrennen

mentor
Eine Klasse besser.

Die Autorin: Verena Rotter, Lehrerin für Englisch, Kunsterziehung, Werken und Technisches Zeichnen

Redaktion: Ulrike Timmer

Illustrationen: Henning Schöttke, Kiel

Umwelthinweis: Gedruckt auf chlorfrei gebleichtem Papier

Layout: Peter Glaubitz, auf der Basis des Layouts von Barbara Slowik, München

Inhaltsverzeichnis

Unser Tipp für alle, die noch mehr wissen wollen:

mentor Lernhilfen

Die sind Spezialisten im Erklären und machen fit fürs ganze Schuljahr!

Für Englisch in der 7./8. Klasse gibt's die Bände:

Grammatik und Wortschatz:
Vertiefung der Grundlagen, Teil 1
ISBN 3-580-63545-X

Grammatik und Wortschatz:
Vertiefung der Grundlagen, Teil 2
ISBN 3-580-63546-8

Vorwort

Hallo, liebe Schülerin, lieber Schüler,

du möchtest dein Englisch ein bisschen trainieren, aber möglichst gezielt und mit Erfolg? Dann bist du hier richtig – egal, ob du dich nun generell verbessern oder eines der Themen dieses Buches speziell üben willst.

Und so funktioniert's:

Treffsicher Dieses Buch ist in **24 kleine Lernportionen** gegliedert.
→ So findest du dich besonders schnell zurecht.

Übersichtlich Jede Lernportion umfasst genau eine **Doppelseite**.
→ So hast du immer alles auf einen Blick.

Einleuchtend Jede Doppelseite beginnt mit einer kurzen, klaren **Regel**.
→ So weißt du immer sofort, worauf es ankommt.

Clever Dann geht's ans **Üben** – ganz locker, Schritt für Schritt.
→ So bereitest du dich optimal vor.

Praktisch Der **Lösungsteil** zum Heraustrennen passt seitengetreu dazu.
→ So kontrollierst du blitzschnell – ohne Suchen und Blättern.

Am besten gleich loslegen!

Viel Spaß und ganz viel Erfolg wünscht dir dein mentor Verlag

Noch ein Tipp Du hast noch mehr Nachholbedarf, aber keine Lust auf Nachhilfe? Dann versuch's doch mit den **mentor Lernhilfen**: Schau mal auf die Seite gegenüber!

A Futurformen

Im Englischen gibt es eine Reihe verschiedener Möglichkeiten, zukünftige Geschehen auszudrücken. Welche Zukunftsform man verwendet, hängt davon ab, ob es sich z. B. um ein schon länger geplantes Vorhaben oder um einen spontanen Entschluss, einen offiziellen Zeitplan oder eine persönliche Verabredung handelt.

1. Will-future für Vermutungen und Vorhersagen

Verwendung

a) für Vorhersagen → *The weather will be nice tomorrow.*

b) für Vermutungen → *I think Dad will be late today.*

Bildung:

bejahter Satz

will + Grundform (Kurzform: *'ll*) → *Dinner will be ready in twenty minutes.*

verneinter Satz

will + *not* + Grundform (Kurzform: *won't*) → *We won't have soup today.*

Fragesatz

(Fragewort +) *will* + Subjekt + Grundform → *Will Ben pass his driving test?*

Merke

Signalwörter

a) *tomorrow, in (3 weeks), next (summer), in (2007)*

b) *I think, I'm sure, probably, perhaps*

Übung 1

Familie Parker aus Reading lauscht dem Wetterbericht. Wie wird das Wetter morgen in Großbritannien? Setze die richtige Verbform ein.

Tomorrow it .... (be) warm and sunny in South England. There .... (be) light winds from the South-West only.

The Midlands .... (be) cloudy, but it .... (stay) dry.

It ………… (rain) heavily in Scotland tomorrow.

In the Highlands there ………… (be) strong winds from the North-West and the temperature there ………… (not go) above 8°C.

In Wales it ………… (be) cloudy, but it ………… (not rain) all day.

You ………… (even, have) some sunny spells *(dt. sonnige Abschnitte)* in the early evening.

In Northern Ireland it ………… (be) cloudy with lots of rain.

Temperatures ………… (not climb) above 10°C.

Übung 2

Die 13-jährige Sarah Parker schreibt einen Aufsatz zum Thema *„When I'm thirty"*. Bilde aus ihrer „Stoffsammlung" Sätze.

earn lots of money → I will ………… .

have husband and children → ………… .

have to cook dinner for my family → ………… .

not have to be at home at 8 p.m. → ………… .

not go to bed at 10 p.m. → ………… .

my parents be over 60 → ………… .

Übung 3

Sarahs deutsche Brieffreundin Laura will von einer berühmten englischen Wahrsagerin Auskünfte über ihre Zukunft … Übersetze ihre Fragen ins Englische.

1. Werde ich mich bald verlieben *(engl. fall in love)*?

…………

2. Werde ich gute Noten bekommen?

…………

3. Wird Petra wirklich aus München wegziehen?

…………

4. Werde ich ein Snowboard zu meinem Geburtstag bekommen?

…………

2. Will-Future für spontane Entschlüsse und Angebote

Verwendung

c) für spontane Entschlüsse, die erst im Moment des Sprechens gefasst werden	*(A: Oh, I forgot the milk.)* → *B: No problem, I'll go and buy some.*
d) für Angebote und Vorschläge: *shall* (dt. sollen) → wird nur mit *I* und *we* verwendet!	→ *Shall I open the window?* *Shall we go swimming today?*
e) nach bestimmten Verben, die in die Zukunft weisen, z. B. *expect, hope, promise, wonder, suppose* (dt. annehmen)	→ *I promise I'll be back at 9 p.m.*

Beachte:
Das englische will-Future wird im Deutschen oft mit dem Präsens wiedergegeben:
I'll go and buy some bread. → Ich geh' und kaufe etwas Brot.

Nicht verwechseln:
I will go now. ↔ *I want to go now.*
Ich werde jetzt gehen. / Ich gehe jetzt. ↔ Ich will jetzt gehen.

Übung 1

Am *Mother's Day* wollen Sarah, Steve und Ben Parker ihrer Mutter jeden Wunsch erfüllen. Schwester Julie ist krank und könnte die Überraschung verderben.
Finde das passende Verb und setze es in die richtige Form.
buy – do – sit – stay – go

1. Mrs Parker: "Look at all these dirty dishes ..."

   Sarah: "I .... the washing-up for you, Mum."

2. Mrs Parker: "We haven't got any biscuits."

   Ben: "No problem, Mum, I .... and buy some."

3. Mrs Parker: "Yesterday I dropped my favourite bottle of perfume on the floor and broke it."
   Ben & Steve: "We .... a new bottle for you."

4. Mrs Parker: "I'd like to go out with Fred tonight, but Julie is ill ..."

   Sarah & Steve: "We .... at home and we .... at her bedside all night, Mum."

Übung 2

Übersetze ins Deutsche, was Mrs Parker noch zu Steve und Sarah sagt, als sie und ihr Mann abends das Haus verlassen.

1. I promise we'll return at 11 p.m.

   ....

2. I hope there won't be a traffic jam *(dt. Stau).*

   ....

3. I suppose Julie's temperature won't rise any (hier: *dt. noch)* further *(dt. weiter).*

   ....

4. I expect Julie will fall asleep soon.

   ....

Übung 3

Als Mr und Mrs Parker weggegangen sind, machen Sarah und Steve der 8-jährigen Julie ein paar Vorschläge, was sie machen könnten. Was haben sie auf Englisch gesagt?

1. Julie: „Mir ist so langweilig. Was sollen wir heute Abend machen?"

   "I'm so bored. ...."

2. Sarah: „Soll ich dir eine Tasse Tee holen?"

   ....

3. Steve: „Soll ich den Fernseher anmachen?"

   ....

4. Sarah & Steve: „Sollen wir dir eine Geschichte vorlesen?"

   ....

5. Steve: „Soll ich dein Malbuch *(engl. colouring book)* bringen?"

   ....

Übung 4

Sarah will in einem Brief „testen", ob Laura schon die verschiedenen Aspekte des will-Future kennt. Kannst du ihr bei der Zuordnung helfen?

1. Shall we go to the cinema tonight?
2. I wonder what the film will be like.
3. There will be seven billion *(dt. Milliarden)* people on our planet soon.
4. A: I like this sweater. – B: I'll buy it for you.
5. I think Sarah will get a good mark in her German test.

a) Vorhersage
b) Vermutung
c) spontanes Angebot
d) Vorschlag
e) will-Future nach bestimmten Verben

A 3. Going to-Future

Verwendung

- für feste, bereits länger bestehende Pläne, Absichten und Vorsätze → *We're going to visit Grandma on Sunday.*
- für absehbare Ereignisse (Anzeichen sind vorhanden) → *(Look at these black clouds.) It is going to rain soon.*

Bildung:

bejahter Satz
am / are / is + going to + Grundform → *Steve is going to learn canoeing in the summer holidays.*

verneinter Satz
am / are / is + not + going to + Grundform → *I'm not going to do the washing-up alone again.*

Fragesatz
(Fragewort +) *am / are / is +* Subjekt + *going to +* Grundform → *Is Sarah going to stay overnight at Vicky's house?*

Beachte:
Das going to-Future verwendet man nicht bei *come* und *go*. Hier bevorzugt man das Present Progressive (vgl. Kap. 7).
My cousin is coming this afternoon. We are going swimming.

Übung 1

Nach Julie ist Mrs Parker krank geworden. Die Kinder haben nun viel zu erledigen. – Ergänze den Dialog.

Mrs Parker: Steve, have you done the shopping yet?

Steve: Not yet, Mum. I .... (do) it later.

Mrs Parker: Sarah, have you cleaned the rooms yet?

Sarah: I've cleaned Ben and Steve's room as well as mine. But Julie's room looks such a mess. I .... (not clean) it.

Mrs Parker: I've just talked to her. She .... (clean) the room herself.

Sarah: Has she got time to do it? It's her turn to scrub *(dt. schrubben)* the kitchen floor, isn't it?

Mrs Parker: You are right, Sarah. It *is* her turn, but she .... (not scrub) the floor. She said she's still too ill …

Übung 2

Mrs Parker hat einen schlimmen Albtraum. Gleich wird etwas passieren! Vervollständige die Sätze mit dem passenden Verb in der richtigen Form.

flood *(dt. überschwemmen)* **boil over** *(dt. überkochen)* **have** **fall off**

1. Julie has put milk onto the stove. She forgets to turn the hot-plate *(dt. Herdplatte)* off.
   The milk ....
2. Steve and Eric are climbing up an old ladder to pick apples. One rung *(dt. Sprosse)* of the ladder is loose. They .... the ladder.
3. Sarah is running a bath (run a bath, *dt. sich ein Bad einlaufen lassen).*
   She leaves the bathroom and talks to her friend Vicky on the phone for an hour.
   The water .... the whole house.
4. Ben is driving a car without a driver's licence *(dt. Führerschein).* He hasn't slept for 24 hours. He .... an accident.

Übung 3

Sarah und ihr Zwillingsbruder Steve werden bald 14.
Laura möchte wissen, wie sie feiern werden.
Kannst du ihr helfen den Brief auf Englisch zu verfassen?

Liebe Sarah, in deinem letzten Brief hast du geschrieben, dass du zusammen mit Steve eine große Party geben wirst …	Dear Sarah, You wrote in your last letter that you .... a big party together with Steve …
Wo werdet ihr feiern *(engl. celebrate)*? Wen wirst du einladen *(engl. invite)*?	Where ....
Welche Musik werdet ihr spielen?	What kind of music ....?
Wird deine Mutter wieder ihre köstlichen Salate machen?	.... her delicious salads again?
Was wirst du Steve zum Geburtstag schenken (= geben)? Ich wünschte, ich könnte mit euch feiern. Deine Laura	.... Steve for his birthday? I wish I could celebrate with you. Yours, Laura

4. Will-Future und going to-Future im Vergleich

Verwendung:

will-Future

- für spontane Entschlüsse (die Entscheidung fällt im Moment des Sprechens)

A: *This is a beautiful sweater.*
B: *I'll buy it for you.*

- für zukünftige Ereignisse, die man nicht beeinflussen kann
  It will rain tomorrow.
  The twins will be 14 next week.
- für reine Vermutungen
  I think Steve will like our present.
- für Angebote und Vorschläge
- nach bestimmten Verben

going to-Future

- für länger gehegte Pläne (die Entscheidung fiel schon vor dem Moment des Sprechens)
  I'm going to buy a pair of shoes this afternoon.
- für zukünftige Ereignisse, die man selbst bestimmen kann
  Sarah is going to visit her grandma tomorrow.
- für absehbare Ereignisse (Anzeichen sind vorhanden)
  Tom has been too lazy.
  He is going to fail his exams.

Merke

Signalwörter:

will-Future

- *probably, perhaps, I think, I'm sure*
- Textzusammenhänge, die deutlich machen, dass die Entscheidung erst im Moment des Sprechens gefällt wird

going to-Future

- Textzusammenhänge, die darauf hinweisen, dass die Entscheidung schon vorher getroffen wurde

Übung 1

Welche Pläne hast du für heute Abend, nächstes Wochenende und die Ferien? Wie sieht's mit deinen Eltern, Freunden und Geschwistern aus? Bilde Sätze.

I my parents my brother / my sister my friend	watch TV / read ? play ? visit ? ?	tonight next weekend in the holidays

1. ....

2. ....

3. ……………………………………………………………………

4. ……………………………………………………………………

5. ……………………………………………………………………

6. ……………………………………………………………………

7. ……………………………………………………………………

Übung 2

Sarah und Steve brauchen noch ein paar „*helping hands*" für ihre Party. Ein paar Freunde bieten spontan ihre Hilfe an. Welche Futurform passt hier?

1. Sarah: "We haven't got enough biscuits."

   Vicky: "I …………………………… (bake) some."

2. Steve: "We've only got fifteen CDs."

   Joe: "I …………………………… (bring) my CD collection."

3. Sarah: "Oh no! I've dropped the chocolate cake!"

   Karen & Amy: "Never mind. We …………………………… (make) a new one."

4. Steve: "Look! We've only got twenty glasses. We need another ten or twelve."

   Susan: "No problem. I …………………………… (go) and get you twenty if you like."

Übung 3

Vor der Party unterhalten sich Freunde von Steve und Sarah. Bilde Sätze in der wörtlichen Rede. Verwende die richtigen Futurformen.

1. Karen fragt Vicky, ob sie denkt, dass Sarah ihr Geschenk gefallen wird.

   Karen: "Vicky, …………………………………………… our present?"

2. Vicky ist sich sicher, dass sie es lieben wird.

   Vicky: "I …………………………………………… it."

3. Eric fragt Justin, was er Steve schenken (= geben) wird.

   Eric: "What …………………………………………… Steve?"

4. Justin antwortet, dass er ihm ein Poster von Andre Agassi schenken wird.

   Justin: "I …………………………………………… a poster of Andre Agassi."

5. Justin fügt hinzu, dass er annimmt, dass Steve es sich an die Wand hängen wird.

   Justin: "I …………………………………………… onto the wall."

5. Will-Future und going to-Future: Mixed Exercises

Übung 1

Mr und Mrs Parker sind auch zur Party gekommen und machen eine Reihe von Vorschlägen und Angeboten. Bilde Sätze.

1. Vicky: "It's really hot in here."

   Mrs Parker: "………………………… (I, open, window)?"

2. Sarah: "I've been dancing for two hours. I'm completely exhausted."

   Mr Parker: "………………………… (I, get, you, chair)?"

3. Steve: "I think we're running out of lemonade."

   Mr & Mrs Parker: "………………………… (we, go) and get some more?"

4. Eric: "I hate this techno music."

   Mr Parker: "………………………… (I, play) one of my Beatles cassettes?"

5. Amy: "I have to be home at 10 p.m. But my parents can't collect me because they haven't got a car this week."

   Mrs Parker: "………………………… (I, drive, you, home)?"

6. Sarah: "Karen would like to stay overnight."

   Mrs Parker: "………………………… (I, make, guest bed) for her?"

Übung 2

Sarah und Steve haben von ihrer Großmutter zum Geburtstag Geld bekommen. Als sie zwei Wochen später wieder kommt, möchte sie wissen, was Sarah und Steve damit vorhaben. Verwende die richtigen Futurformen.

Grandma: Well, Steve and Sarah, what ………………………… (you, do) with the money I gave you?

Sarah: I've already decided that I ………………………… (save) half of it.

Grandma: And what about the other half?

Sarah: I haven't had the time to spend it yet, but I ………………………… (definitely, buy) the brand new *Spice Girls* CD.

Grandma: And what ………………………… (you, do) with the rest?

Sarah: I ………………………… (give) Mum and Dad tickets for the theatre because they helped us so much with our party.

Grandma: That's very nice of you, Sarah. And what ………………………… (you, do) with the money, Steve?

Steve: Well, unlike Sarah, I ………………………… (certainly, not, save) any of it.

Grandma: What ………………………… (you, buy) then?

Steve: I haven't thought about it so far. Perhaps I ………………………… (buy) a pair of new tennis shoes. I hope I ………………………… (find) nice ones. And tomorrow I ………………………… (do) a cycling tour with James and Eric. I'm sure I ………………………… (need) some money.

Grandma: Have you listened to the weather forecast?

Steve: Yes, I have. It ………………………… (be) cloudy but it ………………………… (not, rain).

Übung 3

Hier kommt der Expertentest:
Kannst du jeweils begründen, warum das Futur mit *will / shall* bzw. *going to* gebildet werden muss?

1. It will be rather cold tomorrow. → Vorhersage → *will*
2. Shall we go swimming? → …………………………
3. I'm going to watch a video tonight. → …………………………
4. I promise I'll be back in 5 minutes. → …………………………
5. Look at the sky. It's going to rain. → …………………………
6. I think Ben will pass the test easily. → …………………………
7. (A: I'm too tired to do the shopping.)
   B: No problem. I'll do it for you. → …………………………

A 6. Simple Present mit zukünftiger Bedeutung

Mit dem Simple Present kann man nicht nur regelmäßige Handlungen in der Gegenwart zum Ausdruck bringen, man verwendet es auch, um über bereits festgelegte zukünftige Ereignisse zu sprechen.

Verwendung	
• für zukünftige Geschehen, die durch Fahr- und sonstige Zeitpläne, Kalender, Programme etc. festgelegt sind	→ *Mrs Parker's train leaves at 4.30 p.m.*
→ typische Verben hierfür sind: *arrive, begin, close, end, finish, leave, open, start, stop*	→ *He arrives in Birmingham at 6.30 p.m.*
• in Nebensätzen der Bedingung (Typ I) und der Zeit, die sich auf die Zukunft beziehen (im Hauptsatz → *will-future*)	→ *If the weather is nice tomorrow, Steve and his friends will enjoy their cycling tour.*
→ Konjunktionen: *if, when, while, before, as soon as, not … until*	→ *Steve will phone his parents as soon as they get to the youth hostel.*
Bildung	
Verb in der Grundform	→ *The museums close at 4 p.m.*
bei der 3. Pers. Sing.: + -*(e)s*	→ *The film finishes at 9.30 p.m.*
Beachte:	
Umschreibung mit *do / does* in Frage und Verneinung	→ *When does the museum open?*

Merke

Signalwörter
Datums- und Zeitangaben, z. B. *on (May 17th), at (4 o'clock)*

Übung 1

Steve und seine Freunde wollen mit dem Bus in die Stadt. Ergänze ihre Unterhaltung mit Mr Hill, dem Herbergsvater.

Steve: Excuse me, Mr Hill, when .... the next bus to the city centre .... (leave)?

Mr Hill: It .... (leave) in about ten minutes. What are you going to visit?

Eric: Well, first of all we'd like to go on a sight-seeing tour. Do you know where the tours start?

Mr Hill: They .... (start) in front of the town hall on the hour.

Steve: And I'd like to go to the *British Handcraft Museum.*

Mr Hill: You'll have to hurry then, boys. The museum .... (close) at 4 o'clock.

Eric: And when .... (it, open) tomorrow morning? Just in case we don't manage to get there in time …

Mr Hill: I think it .... (open) at 9 a.m. I can check that for you. Why don't you go to the inline-disco tonight?

James: Inline-disco? Great! Where .... (it, take place, *dt. stattfinden)* and when .... (it, begin)?

Mr Hill: It's in the sports centre in Beechwood Road. And it .... (start) at 8 p.m. and .... (finish) at 11 p.m. But don't forget that the youth hostel .... (close) at 10.30 p.m.

Übung 2

Bilde Sätze mit den angegebenen Konjunktionen.
Achte auf die richtige Zeitform in Haupt- und Nebensatz.

1. Steve / go to bed / as soon as / he / return / from the cycling tour

....

....

2. Sarah / take a shower / before / she / go to the cinema

....

....

3. Mr Parker / phone / his wife / when / he / arrive in Birmingham

....

....

4. The children / not / start / breakfast / until / their parents / sit down at the table

....

....

A 7. Present Progressive mit zukünftiger Bedeutung

Das Present Progressive kann nicht nur gerade ablaufende Handlungen beschreiben, es kann auch Zukünftiges ausdrücken.

Verwendung

- für feste Verabredungen und Pläne in der (nahen) Zukunft → *Steve is playing tennis tomorrow morning.*

Bildung:

bejahter Satz
am / are / is + Grundform + *-ing* → *Ben is watching TV tonight.*

verneinter Satz
am / are / is + *not* + Grundform + *-ing* → *Mr and Mrs Parker aren't watching the film tonight.*

Fragesatz
(Fragewort +) *am / are / is* + Subjekt + *Grundform* + *-ing* → *What time is Sarah meeting Vicky tomorrow?*

Merke

Signalwörter
Zeitangaben oder Zeitadverbien der Zukunft, z. B. *tomorrow, next (week), at (8 o'clock / 9.30 p.m.), on (Wednesday) …*

Übung 1

Was haben die Parkers in der kommenden Woche vor? Bilde Sätze im Present Progressive. Verwende, falls nicht angegeben, die Verben *go (to), take (to), have* oder *play*.

	Mr Parker	Mrs Parker	Ben	Sarah	Steve	Julie
Mon						ballet class
Tue					tennis	
Wed	dentist			visit Karen		
Thu			cinema			
Fri	car / garage		basketball			art class
Sat		meet Liz		shopping	tennis	
Sun						walk dog

1. Mr Parker ………………………………………… on Wednesday.
   He ………………………………………… on Friday.
2. Mrs Parker ………………………………………… her friend Liz on Saturday.
3. Ben ………………………………………… on Thursday evening.
   On Friday he ………………………………………….

4. Sarah .... on Wednesday afternoon.

She .... on Saturday.

5. Steve .... on Tuesday and Saturday.

6. Julie .... a ballet class on Monday and an art class on Thursday.

On Sunday she .... Mrs Pearson's dog.

Übung 2

Samstag Vormittag bei den Parkers …
Vervollständige den Dialog mit den richtigen Verbformen.

Julie: Mum, Jackie has just called. She .... (go swimming) in the afternoon. Can you drive me to the pool?

Mrs Parker: I'm sorry, but I can't. I .... (meet) Liz at 3 p.m.

Julie: What about Dad? He surely .... (not, join) you and Liz, is he?

Mrs Parker: Of course not. But he is busy, too. He .... (put up) new shelves *(dt. Regale)* in his study *(dt. Arbeitszimmer)*.

Julie: That's too bad. But Ben could take me on his motorbike, couldn't he?

Mrs Parker: You needn't ask him, Julie. He's just told me that he and Emma .... (watch) videos in the afternoon.

Why .... (you, not, go) by bike?

Julie: It's got a puncture *(dt. Platten)*, Mum.

Übung 3

Was hast du für die nächste Zeit schon vor bzw. ausgemacht?
Bilde Sätze im Present Progressive.

1. I .... this afternoon.

2. I .... tonight.

3. My best friend and I .... at the weekend.

4. I .... next week.

8. Gegenwartsformen mit zukünftiger Bedeutung im Vergleich

Verwendung:

Present Progressive
- für Pläne und zukünftige Verabredungen, die man selbst festgesetzt hat

  Mr and Mrs Parker are going to the theatre tonight.

Simple Present
- für Pläne und zukünftige Ereignisse, die „offiziell" festgelegt sind, wie z. B. Fahrpläne und Programme

  The performance starts at 8 p.m.

Nicht vergessen:
Verlaufsformen können nur von Tätigkeitsverben gebildet werden!

Beachte:
Für die Verwendung der Gegenwartsformen mit zukünftiger Bedeutung gibt es keine eindeutigen Signalwörter.
Achte daher auf den Text- bzw. Satzzusammenhang, um herauszufinden, ob es sich um „offizielle" oder um eigene Pläne handelt!

Übung 1

Sam, ein Junge aus Sarahs Klasse, möchte sich mit Sarah verabreden. – Welche Gegenwartsform mit zukünftiger Bedeutung passt hier? Setze die richtige Verbform ein.

Sam: Hi, Sarah. Would you like to go to the cinema with me tonight?

Sarah: I'd love to, but I can't. I .... (play) tennis with Steve at 7 p.m.

Sam: That's a pity. How about tomorrow?

Sarah: I'm sorry, but Julie and I .... (visit) our grandparents tomorrow evening.

Sam: What about Thursday evening then?

Sarah: I think that's not possible either. On Thursday I .... (help) my parents in the garden. You know, there's so much to do in spring time.

But are *you* free on Friday? Vicky and I .... (go) to the cinema Friday night. You can join us if you like.

Sam: Of course I do …

Übung 2

Es ist Freitag Abend. Sarah, Vicky und Sam haben sich bei den Parkers getroffen und diskutieren noch. – Verwende die passende Gegenwartsform mit zukünftiger Bedeutung.

Sarah: Well, which film would *you* like to watch, Vicky?

Vicky: I'd like to watch *American Beauty*.

Sam: When .... (it, start)?

Vicky: It .... (start) at 8 o'clock in the *City House* and at 10 o'clock in the *Odeon*.

Sam: And what time .... (the film, finish)?

Vicky: Well, it .... (last, *dt. dauern)* 90 minutes, so it .... (finish) at about 9.30 in the *City House* and at 11.30 in the *Odeon*.

Sarah: The last bus .... (leave) at 11.15, which means that we can't watch it in the *Odeon*. And we really have to hurry if we want to make it in time for the 8 o'clock performance. It's already 7.25.

Sam: When .... (next bus, leave)?

Sarah: It .... (leave) at 7.30 and it .... (arrive) at the cinema at 7.50. Well, hurry up, folks …

Übung 3

**Sarah und Steve gehen nächste Woche auf Klassenfahrt. Laura telefoniert mit Sarah und möchte noch einiges wissen.
Bilde Sätze in der wörtlichen Rede.
Verwende Gegenwartsformen mit zukünftiger Bedeutung.**

Laura möchte wissen …

1. wohin sie fahren — "Where ....?"
2. wie lange sie bleiben — ....
3. ob sie mit dem Reisebus *(engl. coach)* oder dem Zug fahren — ....
4. wann ihr Zug abfährt — ....
5. wann er in Bath ankommt — ....
6. wo sie übernachten (= bleiben) — ....

A 9. Future Progressive

Im Englischen gibt es nicht nur in der Gegenwart und Vergangenheit eine Verlaufsform, sondern auch in der Zukunft.

Verwendung

- für Handlungen, die zu einem bestimmten Zeitpunkt in der Zukunft gerade ablaufen werden → *Mr Parker will be having a meeting tomorrow at 10 o'clock.*
- für Zukunftspläne und Beschreibungen von zukünftigen Geschehen → *This time next week Sarah will be sitting on the train to Bath.*
- für höfliche Fragen, die sich auf die Zukunft beziehen → *Will you be using your computer tomorrow?*

Bildung:

bejahter Satz
will + *be* + Grundform + *-ing* → *Sarah and Steve will be spending a week in Bath.*

verneinter Satz
won't + *be* + Grundform + *-ing* → *Ben won't be watching TV at 7 o'clock.*

Fragesatz
(Fragewort +) *will* + Subjekt + *be* + Grundform + *-ing* → *What will you be doing this weekend?*

Merke

Signalwörter
tonight, tomorrow, next (week), this time next (week) sowie Datums- und Zeitangaben, z. B. *at (11 a.m.), on (November 15th)*

Übung 1

Hier siehst du einen Auszug aus Mr Parkers Terminkalender. Sind die folgenden Aussagen wahr oder falsch? Kreuze an.

9.30–1.00	Meet new team assistant
11.00–1.00	Discuss new project
1.00–2.00	Lunch with Mr Donovan
3.15–4.00	See Mr Jackson
4.00–5.00	Have sales talk *(dt. Verkaufsgespräch)*

	true	false
1. Mr Parker will be having lunch at 2.30 p.m.	○	○
2. Mr Parker will be discussing the new project at 11.30 a.m.	○	○
3. Mr Parker will be meeting the new team assistant at 9 a.m.	○	○
4. Mr Parker will be seeing Mr Jackson before lunch.	○	○
5. Mr Parker will be having a sales talk in the afternoon.	○	○

Übung 2

Sarah träumt schon von der Klassenfahrt nach Bath. Bilde Sätze im Future Progressive.

Next week …

1. … I .... (sleep) in a youth hostel.
2. … Mum .... (not prepare) breakfast for me.
3. … Vicky, Karen and I .... (have) breakfast together.
4. … we .... (visit) the famous Roman baths.
5. … I .... (send) a postcard to Laura from Bath.
6. … Sam and Daniel .... (live on) cheeseburgers.
7. … Steve .... (not play) tennis.
8. … I .... (talk to) Vicky for hours.
9. … I .... (not sleep) at 10.30 p.m.
10. … Steve and I .... (miss) our parents.

Übung 3

Wie du sicher weißt, sind die Briten immer sehr auf Höflichkeit bedacht. Kannst du die folgenden Fragen im Future Progressive bilden?

1. Was machst du heute Abend?

....

2. Wirst du dir morgen das Tennisspiel anschauen?

....

3. Verwendest du nächste Woche dein Lexikon *(engl. dictionary)*?

....

4. Wann wirst du heute Nachmittag das Haus verlassen?

....

5. Wirst du vor 11 Uhr zurückkommen?

....

6. Wann werdet ihr heute zu Abend essen?

....

A 10. Future Perfect

Verwendung • für Ereignisse, die zu einem bestimmten Zeitpunkt in der Zukunft abgeschlossen sein werden	→ *Julie will have finished her homework in ten minutes.*
Bildung: **bejahter Satz** *will* + *have* + 3. Form d. Verbs	→ *Next month Mr Parker will have worked in this firm for ten years.*
verneinter Satz *won't* + *have* + 3. Form	→ *Laura won't have received Sarah's postcard by the time Sarah gets home.*
Fragesatz (Fragewort +) *will* + Subjekt + *have* + 3. Form	→ *When will you have finished your book?*

Merke

Signalwörter
by (dt. bis) *tomorrow / (7) o'clock / next (Friday) …*
not … until (dt. nicht vor) *next (Sunday) / (10) o'clock …*
in (twenty) minutes / hours …, next (week / month) …, when?

Übung 1

Bald sind es zehn Jahre, dass Mr Parker als Programmierer bei *Top-Soft* arbeitet. Was wird er bis zu seinem Jubiläum alles geleistet haben? Bilde Sätze im Future Perfect.

1. Next month Mr Parker .... (work) about two thousand days in this company.
2. He .... (spend) about three thousand hours on trains, buses and planes.
3. He .... (talk) to more than a thousand different customers.
4. He .... (develop) more than eighty computer programmes.
5. He .... (give) about 250 lectures (give a lecture, *dt. einen Vortrag halten).*
6. He .... (travel) to forty European cities.

Übung 2

Morgen steht bei den Parkers wieder der Frühjahrsputz an. Wann wird was von wem (noch nicht) erledigt sein? Bilde Frage- und Antwortsätze im Future Perfect.

	Mr & Mrs Parker	Ben & Steve	Sarah & Julie
9.00–11.00	paint front door	vacuum[1] carpets	——
11.00– 1.00	——	scrub floors	clean cupboards
2.00– 4.00	take curtains down	——	dust[2] furniture

[1] vacuum, *dt. staubsaugen*
[2] dust, *dt. abstauben*

1. .... Mr and Mrs Parker .... the front door by 11 o'clock? – Yes, they .... it by 11 o'clock.
2. .... they .... the curtains down by 3 o'clock? – No, they .... them down until 4 o'clock.
3. .... Ben and Steve .... the carpets by 12 o'clock? – ....
4. .... they .... the floors by 12 o'clock? – .... them until 1 o'clock.
5. .... Sarah and Julie .... the cupboards by 12 o'clock? – ....
6. .... they .... the furniture by 6 o'clock ? – ....

Übung 3

Übersetze ins Englische.

1. Die Parkers werden den Frühjahrsputz *(engl. spring-cleaning)* bis 16 Uhr beendet haben.

....

2. Nächsten Monat werden die Parkers seit 20 Jahren hier wohnen.

....

3. Wird Mr Parker das Haus bis 8 Uhr verlassen haben?

....

A 11. Futurformen im Überblick

Futurform	Verwendung
will-Future	• für Vorhersagen und Vermutungen • für Angebote und Vorschläge *(→ shall)* • für spontane Entschlüsse • nach bestimmten Verben
going to-Future	• für feste Absichten und Pläne • für Ereignisse, für die es Anzeichen gibt
Simple Present	• für zukünftige Geschehen, die durch Zeitpläne oder Programme festgelegt sind • in Nebensätzen der Zeit oder Bedingung
Present Progressive	• für Verabredungen und Pläne in der nahen Zukunft
Future Progressive	• für Handlungsabläufe in der Zukunft • für Zukunftspläne und zukünftige Geschehen • für höfliche Fragen (bzgl. der Zukunft)
Future Perfect	• für Ereignisse, die zu einem zukünftigen Zeitpunkt bereits vorbei sein werden

Übung 1

Bist du noch fit?
Bilde zu den Verben die angegebenen Futurformen.

buy	going to-Future	(bejaht) (Frage)	I .... you ....?
do	Future Perfect	(bejaht) (verneint)	he .... we ....
arrive	Simple Present	(Frage) (verneint)	.... it ....? it ....
lie	Future Progressive	(bejaht) (Frage)	she .... they ....?

rain	will-Future	(Frage) (verneint)	.... it ....? it ....
stay	Present Progressive	(bejaht) (Frage)	I .... he ....?

Übung 2

**Als Futur-Profi könntest du die folgenden Situationen sicher auch auf Englisch meistern.
Welches ist die passende Futurform bei den unterstrichenen Sätzen? Kannst du deine Entscheidung begründen?**

1. Beim Stadtbummel: „Das ist ja ein tolles T-Shirt! Das kauf' ich mir!"

   Futurform im Englischen: ....

   Begründung: ....

2. Am Bahnschalter: „Wann fährt der nächste Zug nach Köln?"

   Futurform im Englischen: ....

   Begründung: ....

3. Du träumst abends im Bett vor dich hin: „Morgen um diese Zeit sitze ich im Zug."

   Futurform im Englischen: ....

   Begründung: ....

4. Du schaukelst in der Schule ganz wild auf deinem Stuhl.
   Dein Lehrer meint: „Du wirst gleich runterfallen!"

   Futurform im Englischen: ....

   Begründung: ....

5. Du bringst dein kaputtes Fahrrad zum Reparieren und fragst:
   „Wann werden Sie das Rad repariert haben?"

   Futurform im Englischen: ....

   Begründung: ....

6. Eine Freundin möchte wissen, was du morgen machst.
   Du sagst: „Meine Cousine kommt morgen."

   Futurform im Englischen: ....

   Begründung: ....

A 12. Abschlusstest Futurformen

Übung 1

Morgen fahren Steve und Sarah mit ihrer Klasse nach Bath. Sieh dir ihren Tagesablauf an und entscheide, welches Ereignis gerade ablaufen oder bereits vorbei sein wird.

8.30 a.m.	leave Reading	1.00–2.00 p.m.	volleyball
8.30–10.00	train journey *(dt. Zugfahrt)*	2.30	go to the city centre
10.00	arrival at Bath	3.00–4.00	visit Roman baths
10.15–10.45	allocation *(dt. Zuteilung)* of rooms	4.00	coffee break
		4.30–5.30	Museum of Local Art
11.30–12.30	lunch	6.00	return to youth hostel

1. At 8.45 a.m. Steve and Sarah .... (leave) Reading.
   They .... (sit) in the train to Bath.
2. At 10.15 they .... (arrive) in Bath.
3. At 10.30 the allocation of the rooms .... (take place, *dt. stattfinden*).
4. At 12 o'clock everybody .... (have) lunch.
5. At 1.30 p.m. they .... (play) volleyball.
6. By 2.45 the class .... (go) to the city centre.
7. At 3.30 they .... (visit) the Roman baths.
8. At 4 o'clock they .... (have) a coffee break.
9. At 5 o'clock everybody .... (look) at the beautiful art objects in the Museum of Local Art.
10. By 6.30 the class .... (return) to the youth hostel.

Übung 2

Am Abend wird das Programm für den folgenden Tag besprochen. – Hier kommen nun alle Futurformen vor!

Steve: What .... (we, do) tomorrow?

Mr Jackson: Well, tomorrow we .... (go) on a sightseeing tour first.

Emily: When .... (it, start)?

Mr Jackson: The tour .... (start) at 9 o'clock. Our bus .... (leave) from in front of the youth hostel at half past eight and .... (arrive) at the town hall *(dt. Rathaus)* at eight-fifty.

Jenny: What do we have to take with us?

Mrs Leech: I think you .... (need) an umbrella. I've just listened to the weather forecast. Tomorrow it .... (be) cloudy with some showers of rain.

Jenny: Oh no! I have forgotten my umbrella!

Sarah: No problem. I .... (lend) you one. I've got two, you know.

Sam: When .... (tour, finish)?

Mr Jackson: It .... (finish) at 11.30 a.m.

Donna: What .... (do) afterwards?

Mrs Leech: If you want to, you can spend the lunch-break together in groups of three or four.

Daniel: Great! .... *(dt. Sollen wir)* have lunch at McDonald's?

Sam: Good idea, Daniel! .... (you, eat) seven cheeseburgers again?

Daniel: If I have enough time, I .... (be able) to eat eight or more.

Mr Jackson: But don't forget to be back at the town hall at 1 p.m.

Sam: We promise we .... (be) back on time. By this time Daniel .... (surely, finish) his eighth cheeseburger. – Sarah, what .... (you, do) at lunch time?

Sarah: Well, Vicky and I have decided to spend the lunch-break at the river. At 12 o'clock we .... (sit) on a bench in the sunshine.

Sam: But there .... (not, be) any sunshine tomorrow …

Sarah: That's a pity. But I think Vicky and I .... (have) a nice break all the same. Without loads of cheeseburgers!

B If-Sätze

1. Grundlagen

Aufbau

If-Sätze bestehen aus zwei Teilen, nämlich
a) einem Nebensatz *(if-clause / if-Satz)* und
b) einem Hauptsatz *(main clause)*
(a) *If the weather is fine tomorrow,* (b) *we will go swimming.*

Bedingung und Folge

Im *if*-Satz wird eine Bedingung zum Ausdruck gebracht, im Hauptsatz steht die Folge aus dieser Bedingung:
Bedingung: (a) Wenn das Wetter morgen schön ist,
Folge: (b) gehen wir schwimmen.

Stellung und Kommasetzung

Steht der Nebensatz vor dem Hauptsatz, werden die beiden Satzteile durch ein Komma voneinander getrennt.
Der Hauptsatz kann aber auch vor dem *if*-Satz stehen; in diesem Fall wird kein Komma gesetzt:
(b) We will go swimming (a) if the weather is fine tomorrow.

Arten von Bedingungen

Die verschiedenen *if*-Satz-Typen im Englischen ergeben sich aus den unterschiedlichen Arten von Bedingungen:

1. wahrscheinliche oder erfüllte Bedingungen → *If it rains tomorrow, Steve and Eric will play computer games.*
2. unwahrscheinliche oder unmögliche Bedingungen → *If Ben had a lot of money, he would buy a car.*
3. nicht mehr erfüllbare Bedingungen → *If Steve had done his maths homework, his teacher wouldn't have been angry with him.*

Beachte:

Das deutsche „wenn" hat im Englischen unterschiedliche Entsprechungen:

1. *if* (dt. wenn, falls) gibt eine Bedingung an:
   If Sam meets Sarah, he'll invite her to his party.
   (→ Es ist nicht klar, ob Sam Sarah trifft.)
2. *when* (dt. wenn, sobald) nennt einen Zeitpunkt:
   When Sam meets Sarah, he'll invite her to his party.
   (→ Es steht bereits fest, dass Sam Sarah treffen wird.)

Übung 1 **Welcher Satzteil stellt die Bedingung und welcher die Folge dar?**

1. Mr Parker / win / in the lottery	he / buy / a car / for Ben
Bedingung	Folge ....
2. Sarah / go / to Sam's party	he / invite / her
....	....
3. Mrs Parker / be / happy	Julie / help / her / with the housework
....	....
4. Steve / work / harder	he / get / a good mark
....	....
5. Julie and Jackie / not go / to the zoo	it / rain / tomorrow
....	....
6. The Parkers / go on holiday / to Spain	they / have / enough money
....	....

Übung 2 **In welchen der folgenden if-Sätze muss ein Komma stehen? Setze es an die richtige Stelle.**

1. If Mr Parker hurries he'll catch the train.
2. If I were you I would work harder.
3. We can go outside if it stops raining.
4. Can you answer the phone if it rings?
5. If Daniel hadn't eaten eight cheeseburgers he wouldn't have been sick afterwards.
6. Sarah would buy this skirt if it wasn't pink.
7. If you ever go to New York you must visit the *Museum of Modern Art*.
8. Ben would be really unhappy if he didn't pass his driving-test *(dt. Fahrprüfung)*.

Übung 3 **Vervollständige die Sätze mit *if* bzw. *when*.**

1. Sarah will take a hot shower .... she returns from Bath.
2. Laura will get the postcard next Wednesday .... Sarah posts it on Friday.
3. .... Steve were as old as Ben, he could take driving-lessons, too.
4. Ben: "I need more pocket money, Dad ..."
   Mr Parker: "You'll get five pounds .... you mow the lawn *(dt. den Rasen mähen)*." Ben: "O.K., I'll do it .... I've finished my homework."

B 2. Typ I mit will-Future

Verwendung

- für (a) wahrscheinliche oder (b) erfüllte Bedingungen (→ Was ist, wenn …?) → *(a) If Ben passes his driving test, he'll give a big party. (b) If Eric likes tennis, he'll surely watch the match tonight.*

Bildung:

Verb im *if*-Satz	Verb im Hauptsatz
Simple Present *If the sun comes out later,*	will-future *Steve and Eric will play tennis.*

Nicht vergessen:
Vollverben müssen im Simple Present mit *do* bzw. *does* verneint werden → *Mum will get very angry if you don't come immediately.*

Beachte:
Das Simple Present bezieht sich (a) auf die Zukunft bei erfüllbaren Bedingungen oder (b) auf die Gegenwart, wenn gegenwärtig bestehende Zustände ausgedrückt werden (erfüllte Bedingungen). Zustandsverben sind z. B. *be, believe, belong, cost, forget, have got, hate, like, love, remember, seem, understand, want, wish*

Übung 1

Verbinde die Satzhälften zu sinnvollen Sätzen.

1. If Steve doesn't hurry,
2. If you read through the text carefully,
3. Tom will join us at the cinema
4. My mother will be angry with me
5. If you help me with the maths homework,
6. I will return this book to Sue
7. If you bring some sandwiches,

a) I'll help you with the French translation.
b) if I don't help her with the housework.
c) I'll bring some cans of lemonade.
d) if I see her today.
e) he'll miss the bus.
f) you'll be able to answer the questions easily.
g) if you don't mind.

Übung 2

Sam möchte sich mal wieder mit Sarah verabreden. Setze die richtigen Verbformen ein.

Sam: Hi, Sarah. What are you doing at the weekend?

Sarah: If the weather .... (be) nice, Vicky and I .... (go) shopping on Saturday.

Sam: And what .... (you, do) if the weather .... (not be) nice?

Sarah: We .... (probably, not stay) at home even if it .... (not be) sunny. But if it .... (rain), Vicky and I .... (meet) at my place and we .... (prepare) our geography paper *(dt. Referat)* together.

Sam: Do you need some help?

Sarah: If you .... (be) keen on that stuff *(dt. Zeugs)*, we .... (not send) you away.

Sam: What are you doing on Saturday evening? There's a good film at the *Odeon*.

Sarah: Well, my parents are spending a day in London on Saturday. And Julie mustn't be left alone. But if they .... (return) in time, I .... (be able) to join you.

Sam: And if they .... (not come back) in time?

Sarah: Hm ... I've got an idea! If my parents .... (not return) in time, we .... (watch) some videos. Is that okay with you?

Sam: Great! See you tomorrow ...

Übung 3

Was machst du unter folgenden Bedingungen? – Bilde anhand der Stichpunkte englische Bedingungssätze vom Typ I.

1. weather / be / nice / tomorrow

   If the weather .... nice tomorrow, I will ....

2. it / not rain / this afternoon

   ....

3. my friend X / visit / me / on Saturday

   ....

4. my parents / give / me / more pocket money / next month

   ....

   ....

B 3. Typ I mit Imperativ oder modalem Hilfsverb

Verwendung
s. Kap. B 2.

Bildung:

Verb im *if*-Satz	Verb im Hauptsatz
Simple Present *If it rains this afternoon,*	Imperativ *take an umbrella with you.*
Simple Present *If you don't have an umbrella,*	modales Hilfsverb + Grundform *you must stay indoors.* *you can stay indoors.* *you may stay indoors.*

Beachte:

I must ↔ *I needn't* — ich muss ↔ ich muss nicht
I may ↔ *I mustn't* — ich darf ↔ ich darf nicht

Übung 1

Verbinde die Satzhälften zu sinnvollen Sätzen.

1. If the water is too cold,
2. Julie must put on some weight
3. Steve can win the tennis trophy
4. If we don't hurry,
5. If you help me with the washing-up today,
6. You must do your homework on Sunday
7. If a stranger wants you to open the door,
8. Sarah can go to the cinema with Sam

a) you mustn't let him in.
b) if he is in good form tomorrow.
c) if Mr and Mrs Parker return in time.
d) you needn't help me tomorrow.
e) if you don't do it on Friday or Saturday.
f) we can't swim in the lake.
g) we won't see the beginning of the film.
h) if she weighs less than 20 kilos.

Übung 2

Sicher weißt du, welche Sehenswürdigkeiten man in welcher Stadt besichtigen kann (oder unbedingt muss). Bilde Sätze anhand der Vorgaben in der Tabelle.

Paris Vienna London Berlin Florence	can must	visit go to walk along see have a look at	the *Ku'damm*. the *Uffizien*. the *Eiffel Tower*. *St Paul's Cathedral*. the *Hofburg*.

1. If you go to Paris, you ....

2. If you visit Vienna, ...

3. If you ……………………………………………………………………………………………….

4. If ……………………………………………………………………………………………………….

5. …….

Übung 3

Hier musst du nur noch die unterstrichenen Satzteile ins Englische übersetzen.

1. Wenn Julie in der Mathearbeit eine gute Note bekommt, darf sie in den Zoo gehen.

   If Julie gets a good mark in the maths test, she ………………………… to the zoo.

2. Wenn Sarah heute nicht pünktlich zurück ist, darf sie morgen nicht ausgehen.

   If Sarah doesn't come back on time today, ……………………………………………… tomorrow.

3. Wenn Steve nicht um acht Uhr zurück ist, kann er den Film nicht anschauen.

   If Steve isn't back at 8 o'clock, ……………………………………………….

4. Wenn Ben mehr Taschengeld will, muss er seinem Vater im Garten helfen.

   If Ben wants more pocket money, ………………………………………………

   ……………………………………………………………………………………….

5. Wenn die Parkers eine Haushälterin einstellen, braucht Frau Parker nicht die ganze Hausarbeit allein zu machen.

   If the Parkers take on a housekeeper, ………………………………………………

   ……………………………………………………………………………………….

Übung 4

Sarah hat aufgeschrieben, welche Sätze ihrer Eltern sie am meisten nerven. Übersetze sie ins Deutsche.

1. Don't forget your umbrella if it rains.

   ……………………………………………………………………………………….

2. Tidy up your room if you don't find your things.

   ……………………………………………………………………………………….

3. Help me with the housework if you don't have anything better to do.

   ……………………………………………………………………………………….

   ……………………………………………………………………………………….

B 4. Typ I: Mixed Exercises

Verb im *if*-Satz	Verb im Hauptsatz
Simple Present	a) *will*-Future oder b) modales Hilfsverb oder c) Imperativ
If the sun shines tomorrow,	a) *we will play in the garden.* b) *we can play in the garden.* c) *go and play in the garden.*

Übung 1

Sarah möchte Laura in München besuchen.
Laura hat sich schon einiges überlegt.
Hilfst du ihr, den Brief ins Englische zu übersetzen?

Liebe Sarah, hast du dich schon entschieden, wann du kommen möchtest?	Dear Sarah, Have you already decided when to come?
Wenn du im August kommst, ist das Wetter sicher schön.	If you .... in August, the ....
Falls du an den Sehenswürdigkeiten Münchens interessiert bist, können wir eine Stadtführung machen.	If .... interested in the sights of Munich, we .... a sight-seeing tour.
Aber wir müssen (auch) keine machen, wenn du das langweilig findest.	But we .... if .... that's boring.
Wenn du gerne spazieren gehst, müssen wir (unbedingt) zum *Englischen Garten* gehen.	.... going for walks, ... the *Englischer Garten.*
Falls du in München gerne Klamotten kaufen willst, werde ich dir ein paar tolle Geschäfte zeigen.	.... clothes in Munich, ... some fantastic shops.
Ich bin mir sicher, dass wir zusammen eine tolle Zeit haben werden. Schreib bald! Deine Laura	I'm sure that we'll have a great time together. Write soon. Love, Laura

Übung 2

Sam liegt abends in seinem Bett und plant das nächste *date* mit Sarah. – Setze die richtigen Verbformen ein.

1. If I ………… (see) her tomorrow, I ………… (ask) her whether she's got any plans for the weekend.
2. If she ………… (not have) any plans, I ………… (suggest, *dt. vorschlagen)* that we go on a cycling tour.
3. If she ………… (not have) a bike, she ………… (borrow, *können*) my sister's bike.
4. If she ………… (not like) cycling, I ………… (ask) her to go to the cinema with me.
5. If she ………… (want) to go to the cinema, she ………… (choose, *dürfen*) a film she would like to see.
6. If she ………… (choose) a film I've already seen, I ………… (not tell) her.
7. If she really ………… (go) to the cinema with me, I ………… (be) extremely happy.

Übung 3

Hier geht's nun um dich! Setze die fehlenden Bedingungen bzw. Folgen ein, so dass die Sätze auf dich zutreffen.

1. I'll be very happy if …………
2. If I get a good mark in my next English test, my parents …………
3. If my sister / brother uses my computer without asking me, I …………
4. I'll get very angry if …………
5. If it rains tomorrow, I …………
6. I'll be thankful *(dt. dankbar, froh)* if …………

B 5. Typ II mit unwahrscheinlicher Bedingung

Verwendung

- für Bedingungen, die unwahrscheinlich sind (→ Was würde geschehen, wenn …?) → *If Ben won a lot of money, he would buy a car.*

Bildung:

Verb im *if*-Satz	Verb im Hauptsatz
Simple Past	a) Conditional I: *would* + Grundform (Kurzform: *'d*) b) *could / might* + Grundform
If Mr Parker won in the lottery,	a) *he would buy a car for Ben.* b) *he could buy a car for Ben.*

Beachte:

Das Simple Past drückt hier keine Vergangenheit aus, sondern bezieht sich auf die Zukunft → *Steve would be sad if he lost the tennis match tomorrow.* (Es ist aber unwahrscheinlich, dass er es verlieren wird.)

Nicht vergessen:

Vollverben müssen im Simple Past mit *did* verneint werden → *Steve would be sad if he didn't win the tennis match tomorrow.*

Übung 1

Bei den Parkers könnte einiges anders werden, wenn …
Setze die richtigen Verbformen ein.

1. If Sarah ………… (clean) her room more often, it ………… (not look) such a mess.
2. Ben ………… (get) more pocket money if he ………… (help) his father more often in the garden.
3. If Steve ………… (practise, *dt. trainieren)* even harder, he ………… (become) the best tennis player in his school.
4. Julie ………… (have) more time for painting pictures if she ………… (not take) so many ballet classes.

Übung 2

Ben, Sarah, Steve und Julie spielen *Crazy Situations*. In der Tabelle siehst du die gegebenen (unwahrscheinlichen) Situationen sowie die verschiedenen Antworten. Bilde Sätze.

	Ben	**Sarah**	**Steve**	**Julie**
find a snake *(dt. Schlange)* in your bed	kill it	call the police	catch it	scream *(dt. schreien)*
meet an alien	say "hello"	ask its name	not do anything	be afraid

1. If Ben .... a snake in his bed, he .... it.
2. If Sarah .... a snake in her bed, she ....
3. If Steve .... a snake in his bed, ...
4. If Julie .... a snake in her bed, ...
5. If Ben .... an alien, he .... "hello".
6. If Sarah .... an alien, ...
7. If Steve ....
8. If Julie ....

Übung 3

Und was würdest du in diesen Situationen tun? Vervollständige die Sätze und übersetze sie ins Deutsche.

1. If I .... (find) a snake in my bed, I ....

   ....

   Wenn ich eine Schlange ....

   ....

2. If I .... (meet) an alien, I ....

   Wenn ich einen Außerirdischen ....

   ....

B 6. Typ II mit unmöglicher Bedingung

Verwendung

- für Bedingungen, die unmöglich sind, weil sie den gegebenen Tatsachen widersprechen (→ Was wäre, wenn …?)
  → *If Ben had a lot of money, he would buy a car.* (Er hat aber nicht viel Geld!)

Bildung:

Verb im *if*-Satz	Verb im Hauptsatz
Simple Past	*would / could / might* + Grundform

Beachte:

Das Simple Past drückt hier keine Vergangenheit aus, sondern bezieht sich auf die Gegenwart
→ *If I had enough money, I would buy this T-shirt.* (Wenn ich (jetzt) genug Geld hätte …)

Um jemandem einen Rat zu geben, kann man den Ausdruck *If I were you* … verwenden
→ *If I were you, I wouldn't buy these shoes.* (Wenn ich du wäre … / Ich an deiner Stelle …)

Übung 1

Sarah ist heute mal wieder total unzufrieden mit sich selbst und wünscht sich, dass vieles anders wäre.
Setze die richtigen Verbformen ein.
Beachte die Stellung von Bedingung und Folge.

1. If I ………… (have) dark hair, I ………… (look) much better.
2. If I ………… (not have) such short legs, I ………… (wear) mini-skirts.
3. I ………… (be) much happier if my hair ………… (not be) so curly.
4. If I ………… (be) taller, I ………… (wear) these fashionable trousers.
5. I ………… (not be) so self-conscious *(dt. befangen)* if I ………… (not have) so many spots *(dt. Pickel)*.

Übung 2

Steve hat sich in Lucy verliebt und würde sie gerne anrufen, weiß aber ihre Nummer nicht. Er träumt vor sich hin …

1. I / know / Lucy's number, I / phone / her

   If I .... Lucy's number, I .... her.

2. she / not / be / so beautiful, I / dare *(dt. sich etw. trauen)* to tell / her / I love her

   If ....

3. she / be / my girl-friend, I / be / the happiest person in the world

   ....

4. I / have / lots of money, I / buy / her / anything she wants

   ....

Übung 3

Freunde von dir wollen in den folgenden Situationen deinen Rat. Verwende die gegebenen Stichwörter.

1. Friend A: "I look a mess. What shall I do with my hair?" (go / hairdresser's)

   You: "If I .... you, I ...."

2. Friend B: "I lied to my mother. I feel terrible." (tell / her / truth)

   You: "If I ....

3. Friend C: "I've put on weight (put on weight, *dt. zunehmen*)." (do / a lot of sport)

   You: "If ....

4. Friend D: "These trousers look great. But they're too small." (not / buy / them)

   You: ....

Übung 4

Vollende die angefangenen Sätze in deinem Sinne und übersetze sie ins Deutsche.

1. If I were eighteen, I ....

   ....

2. If I were a pop star, ...

   ....

3. If I had lots of money, ...

   ....

B 7. Typ I und Typ II im Vergleich

Typ I

Verwendung
- für wahrscheinliche oder erfüllte Bedingungen

Bildung:

if-Satz	Hauptsatz
Simple Present	will-Future modales Hilfsverb Imperativ

If it rains, Sarah and Sam will watch some videos.
(Auf Grund des Wetterberichts ist mit Regen zu rechnen.)

If it's cold outside, you can't wear shorts.
(Heute ist es kalt draußen.)

Typ II

- für unwahrscheinliche oder unmögliche Bedingungen

if-Satz	Hauptsatz
Simple Past	*would / could / might* + Grundform

↔ *If it didn't rain, Sarah and Sam would go swimming.*
(Es ist unwahrscheinlich, dass es nicht regnet.)

↔ *If it wasn't so cold now, Sarah could wear shorts.*
(Jetzt ist es aber kalt.)

Übung 1

Trage die folgenden if-Sätze in die richtige Spalte der Tabelle ein.

a) Steve and Eric can play tennis if the sun comes out later.
b) If I were you, I wouldn't tell her secrets any more.
c) If the sun shines, we won't stay indoors.
d) What would you do if you met the Queen in the street?
e) If Ben had enough time today, he could help his father in the garden.
f) Tidy up your room if you don't know what else to do.

Typ I	Typ II
....	....
....	....
....	....
....	....
....	....
....	....

Übung 2

Handelt es sich bei den folgenden if-Sätzen um Typ I oder Typ II? Setze die fehlende Verbform ein.

1. If my grandma .... (give) me some money, I can buy a new skateboard.
2. Sarah .... (phone) Laura more often if it was cheaper.
3. If you help me with the washing-up, I .... (clean) your shoes.
4. If I .... (be) you, I would tell my parents the truth.
5. Would you mind if I .... (open) the window?
6. .... (go) to your room if you keep on shouting like this.

Übung 3

Lies dir die folgenden Situationen durch und entscheide, ob die Bedingung erfüllbar ist oder nicht. Setze dann die richtigen Verbformen ein.

1. *Steve is alone in his room. He is thinking …*

   a) If Eric .... (be) here now, we .... (play) tennis.

   b) If he .... (come) later, we .... (play) tennis.

2. *Sarah and Vicky are in a shop. Sarah is trying on (try on,* dt. anprobieren) *a blue dress. She says:*

   a) "I .... (love) to buy this dress if it .... (be) red."

   b) "If I .... (find) a red one in another shop, I .... (buy) it."

3. *It is a warm, sunny day. Ben and Emma are sitting in the garden. Ben is thinking …*

   a) We .... (go) inside if it .... (get) colder later.

   b) If it .... (not be) sunny, we .... (not spend) the day in the garden.

4. *Julie's classmates often laugh at her and call her "little baby", because she still takes her doll to school.*

   a) If Julie .... (not take) her doll to school, they .... (not call) her "little baby".

   b) If she .... (leave) it at home next week, they .... (not laugh) at her any more.

8. Typ III

Verwendung

- für Bedingungen, die in der Vergangenheit nicht gegeben waren, also nicht mehr erfüllbar sind (→ Was wäre gewesen, wenn …?)

→ *If Ben had made one more mistake, he wouldn't have passed the driving-test.* (Er hat aber keinen weiteren Fehler mehr gemacht!)

Bildung:

Verb im *if*-Satz	**Verb im Hauptsatz**
Past Perfect	a) Conditional II: *would* + *have* + 3. Form b) *could* / *might* + *have* + 3. Form
If Steve had known Lucy's phone number, (Er wusste sie aber nicht!)	a) *he would have phoned her.* b) *he could have asked her to visit him.*

Beachte:

Die Kurzform *'d* steht

- im if-Satz für *had* → *If I'd known your number,*
- im Hauptsatz für *would* → *I'd have called you.*

Merke

Signalwörter

Zeitangaben der Vergangenheit, z. B. *yesterday, last (week)* …

Übung 1

Steht *'d* hier für *had* oder für *would*?
Schreibe die volle Form hinter die Kurzform.

1. If Ben had had enough time, he'd have helped = ... his father in the garden.
2. Sarah wouldn't have gone to the cinema if she'd known = ... that it was such a bad film.
3. If he'd felt = ... better, Steve would have won the tennis match.
4. We'd have gone = ... to the theatre if we'd had = ... enough money.

Übung 2

Steve kommt nach seinem verlorenen Spiel nach Hause. Setze die richtigen Verbformen ein.

Mrs Parker: Hi, Steve. How was the match?

Steve: It was awful, Mum. I lost.

Mrs Parker: Never mind, Steve. But what happened?

Steve: It was just too hot. If it .... (not be) so hot, I .... (win) the match.

Mrs Parker: Why is that?

Steve: My hands were wet with sweat. If I .... (not sweat) so much, I .... (hit) more balls.

Mrs Parker: Did you have enough mineral water with you?

Steve: No, just one bottle. If I .... (take) more water with me, I .... (not get) tired so quickly. And to make things worse I even forgot my sunglasses. I'm sure I .... (play) much better if I .... (not forget) my sunglasses.

Mrs Parker: Don't blame it on the sunglasses, Steve. You just had a bad day.

Steve: You're probably right, Mum. If I .... (be) in form, I .... (not lose) the match.

Übung 3

Auch Sarah hatte einen schlechten Tag und überlegt, was anders sein hätte können, wenn … – Bilde *if*-Sätze vom Typ III.

1. I went to bed late last night. That's why I overslept (oversleep, *dt. verschlafen*).

   If I .... to bed earlier, I ....

2. I was hungry all morning, because I didn't have time for breakfast.

   I wouldn't ....

   ....

3. I didn't study enough for the maths test. I couldn't answer all the questions.

   ....

   ....

9. Unmögliche Bedingungen im Vergleich (Typ II und Typ III)

Typ II

Verwendung

- für Bedingungen, die unmöglich sind, weil sie in der Gegenwart nicht erfüllt werden können

Bildung:

if-Satz	Hauptsatz
Simple Past	*would / could / might* + Grundform

If the weather was nice, we would play outdoors.
(Es ist aber nicht schön!)

↔

Typ III

- für Bedingungen, die unmöglich sind, weil sie in der Vergangenheit nicht erfüllt wurden

if-Satz	Hauptsatz
Past Perfect	*would / could / might + have* + 3. Form

If the weather had been nice, we would have played outdoors.
(Es war aber nicht schön!)

Merke

Signalwörter:

Typ II
Zeitangaben der Gegenwart, z. B. *today, now*

↔

Typ III
Zeitangaben der Vergangenheit, z. B. *last (year), yesterday, (two days) ago*

Übung 1

Die folgenden Satzpaare sind nur auf den ersten Blick ähnlich. Handelt es sich um *if*-Sätze des Typs II oder III? Setze die richtige Verbform ein.

1. If Sam had enough money, he .... (buy) a bunch of flowers for Sarah.
2. If Sam had had enough money last week, he .... (buy) a bottle of perfume for Sarah.
3. Ben would be sad if Emma .... (not be) here now.
4. Ben would have been sad if he .... (not pass) his driving-test.
5. Julie .... (paint) some pictures if it had rained yesterday.
6. Julie .... (not sit) in the garden if it was raining now.

Übung 2

Forme die folgenden Sätze in *if*-Sätze vom Typ II bzw. III um.

1. Julie can't draw now because she can't find her pencil.

   If Julie .... her pencil, she .... now.

2. Steve didn't play tennis yesterday because his right leg hurt.

   Steve .... tennis yesterday if ....

   ....

3. Ben doesn't see Emma very often these days because he has such a lot of homework to do.

   ....

   ....

4. Sarah couldn't bake a cake last Sunday because she forgot to buy some eggs.

   ....

   ....

Übung 3

Laura geht seit drei Wochen mit Jonas.
In einem Brief will sie Sarah von ihrem ersten Streit berichten.
Hilfst du ihr beim Übersetzen?

... Wenn ich gestern nicht zu Hause gewesen wäre, hätte er mich (gar) nicht besuchen können. Wenn wir uns nicht getroffen hätten, hätten wir nicht gestritten (streiten, *engl. argue*).	If I .... at home yesterday, he .... me. If ...., we ....
Vielleicht wäre er nicht gegangen, wenn ich ihm zugehört hätte.	He .... if I ....
Jetzt bin ich total unglücklich.	I'm extremely unhappy now.
Was würdest du an meiner Stelle tun? Ich wäre so glücklich, wenn er jetzt hier wäre ...	What ....

10. Typ I, Typ II und Typ III im Vergleich

Verwendung:
Folgende Tabelle zeigt dir den Zusammenhang zwischen Art der Bedingung und zeitlichem Bezug der Bedingung.

	Zukunft	**Gegenwart**	**Vergangenheit**
Typ I	wahrscheinlich	erfüllt	——
Typ II	unwahrscheinlich	unmöglich	——
Typ III	——	——	nicht mehr möglich

Beachte:
Bezieht sich eine Bedingung auf die Zukunft oder Gegenwart, musst du oft aus dem Textzusammenhang erschließen, ob du Typ I oder Typ II verwenden musst.

Bildung:

Typ I	*if*-Satz Hauptsatz	Simple Present will-Future / modales Hilfsverb / Imperativ
Typ II	*if*-Satz Hauptsatz	Simple Past *would* / *could* / *might* + Grundform
Typ III	*if*-Satz Hauptsatz	Past Perfect *would* / *could* / *might* + *have* + 3. Form

Typ I	*If it is warm tomorrow,* *Sarah and Vicky will go swimming.*
Typ II	*If it was warm now,* *Sarah and Vicky would spend the afternoon in the garden.*
Typ III	*If it had been warm yesterday,* *Sarah and Vicky would have done a cycling tour.*

Übung 1

Stelle bei den folgenden if-Sätzen den Satztyp fest.

1. If Julie found a purse in the street, she'd take it to the police. → Typ ....
2. Mr Parker will miss the train if he doesn't hurry. → Typ ....
3. Steve might have won the match if he had been in form. → Typ ....
4. If Ben has got enough money, he'll give a big party next week. → Typ ....
5. If Sarah hadn't forgotten her textbook at school, she would have been able to do her homework. → Typ ....

Übung 2

Bestimme bei den folgenden Sätzen den zeitlichen Bezug, die Art der Bedingung und somit den Typ I, II oder III.
Achte bei der Übersetzung insbesondere auf die Verbformen und die Stellung von Haupt- und Nebensatz.

1. Wenn Sarah zu Hause gewesen wäre, hätte Sam sie ins Kino eingeladen.

   zeitl. Bezug: .... Bedingung: .... Typ ....

   Übersetzung: If Sarah ....

   ....

2. *Der Wetterbericht hat für morgen schönes Wetter und Temperaturen bis zu 27°C vorhergesagt.*
   Wenn es morgen regnen würde, könnten Sarah und Sam kein Picknick machen (ein Picknick machen, *engl. to have a picnic*).

   zeitl. Bezug: .... Bedingung: .... Typ ....

   Übersetzung: ....

   ....

3. Sarah wird ihre neuen Shorts anziehen, falls es morgen richtig heiß wird.

   zeitl. Bezug: .... Bedingung: .... Typ ....

   Übersetzung: ....

   ....

4. Wenn Sam gerne schwimmt, kann er im See ein Bad nehmen *(engl. have a swim)*.

   zeitl. Bezug: .... Bedingung: .... Typ ....

   Übersetzung: ....

   ....

5. *Bevor Sam und Sarah am nächsten Tag losziehen, sagt Mrs Parker zu Sarah:*
   „Ich an deiner Stelle (= Wenn ich du wäre) würde ein Insektenschutzmittel *(engl. insect repellent)* mitnehmen."

   zeitl. Bezug: .... Bedingung: .... Typ ....

   Übersetzung: ....

   ....

B 11. Abschlusstest if-Sätze

Übung 1

Lies dir die folgenden if-Sätze durch und entscheide, welche der beiden Aussagen jeweils zutrifft. Kreuze an!

1. Ben wouldn't go to school by motorbike if it rained tomorrow.
   → ◯ es ist wahrscheinlich, dass es regnet
   ◯ es ist unwahrscheinlich, dass es regnet
2. If Jenny comes to Ben's party, she'll bring a chocolate cake.
   → ◯ mit Jennys Kommen ist zu rechnen
   ◯ mit Jennys Kommen ist nicht zu rechnen
3. Sarah wouldn't have got a bad mark if she had worked harder.
   → ◯ Sarah hat zu wenig für die Schule getan
   ◯ Sarah tut momentan zu wenig
4. If Vicky had known that Sarah was at home, she would have visited her.
   → ◯ Vicky wusste, dass Sarah zu Hause ist
   ◯ Vicky wusste nicht, dass Sarah zu Hause ist
5. Mr Parker could drive Julie to the pool if he was back at 4 p.m.
   → ◯ er wird um 16 Uhr wahrscheinlich zurück sein
   ◯ er wird um 16 Uhr wohl nicht zurück sein

Übung 2

Als Sarah Lauras Brief erhält, ruft sie sie sofort an, um zu erfahren, ob Laura und Jonas sich wieder versöhnt haben.
Setze die richtigen Verbformen ein.

Sarah: Hi, Laura. How are you?

Laura: Hi, Sarah. Not too good. Are you in a hurry?

Sarah: Of course I'm not. I .... (not phone) you if I .... (not have) time. Why are you asking?

Laura: Well, it's quite a long story … Jonas and I had another argument *(dt. Streit)*.

Sarah: Oh dear! What happened?

Laura: I was playing games on Jonas' computer when it suddenly crashed. I really felt sorry. If it .... (not be) me who was playing, it .... (not be) my fault *(dt. Fehler)*.

Sarah: I don't think that's such a big problem. What did Jonas do then?

Laura: He called me a fool. Then I went mad and threw some CDs at him. You know, I .... (not throw) CDs at him if he .... (not call) me a fool.

Sarah: Did they hit him?

Laura: No, the CDs missed him and landed on his bed. I think I .... (feel) sorry if I .... (hurt) him.

Sarah: What did you do then?

Laura: I left at once. And Jonas didn't stop me going.

Sarah: Have you heard anything from him since?

Laura: No, not yet. And I'm sure that he won't phone me. If he .... (phone) and .... (say) he was sorry that he'd called me a fool, everything .... (be) all right again. But I think it's over. What .... (you, do) if you .... (be) me?

Sarah: Well, I think it's not just his fault. If I .... (be) you, I .... (call) him and ask him to forgive me as well.

Laura: Maybe you're right, Sarah. If he .... (not call) me within the next few hours, I .... (call) him. – Just a second, Sarah. The doorbell is ringing. If it .... (be) Jonas, I .... (tell) him that I'm really sorry and that I still love him …

Übung 3

Auch Sarah hat ein Problem: ihre verpatzte Matheschulaufgabe. Kannst du ihren Tagebucheintrag übersetzen?

May 26

I've got a 'D' *(dt. Note 4)* in the maths test. Ugh! If I had worked harder I wouldn't have got such a bad mark. And I might have done better if Mr Summer had explained the subject *(dt. Stoff)* properly *(dt. richtig, anständig)*. Sam said "I wouldn't worry if I were you. You've got enough good marks." Maybe he's right. If I don't get another 'D', there'll be a 'B' *(dt. Note 2)* in my report *(dt. Zeugnis)*.

26. Mai

....
....
....
....
....
....
....
....
....
....

B 12. Sonderformen

Neben den bisher aufgeführten Haupttypen der if-Sätze gibt es – abhängig von Art der Bedingung und zeitlichem Bezug – diverse Sonderformen.
Folgende Varianten können (je nach Bundesland, Schulart und Lehrbuch), müssen aber nicht, Stoff der 7. oder 8. Klasse sein. Abweichungen gegenüber den Haupttypen sind unterstrichen.

Typ I

	if-Satz	Hauptsatz
• wenn die Bedingung bereits erfüllt worden ist	Present Perfect	will-Future modales Hilfsverb Imperativ

→ *If you've been to Rome, you can tell me something about its sights.*

• bei bestehenden Fähigkeiten (→ *can*) oder Verpflichtungen (→ *must*)	modales Hilfsverb (bzw. zugehörige Ersatzverben)	will-Future modales Hilfsverb Imperativ

→ *If you can speak English, you'll be able to translate this.*

• wenn der Verlauf einer Bedingung betont wird	Present Progressive*	will-Future modales Hilfsverb Imperativ

→ *If it's raining, Julie will stay indoors.* * nur bei Tätigkeitsverben!

• wenn eine logische Folge ausgedrückt wird	Simple Present	Simple Present

→ *If you put ice into a hot oven, it melts* (*melt*, dt. schmelzen).

Typ II

• für eine bestehende (irreale) Bedingung mit Folgen für die Vergangenheit	Simple Past	*would / could / might* + *have* + 3. Form

→ *If Vicky's parents had more money, they would have spent their holiday at the seaside.*

Typ III

• für eine (irreale) Bedingung in der Vergangenheit mit Folgen für die Gegenwart	Past Perfect	*would / could / might* + Grundform

→ *If Sarah hadn't spent all her money, she could buy that CD now.*

Übung 1 **Ordne den Sätzen die jeweilige Begründung zu.**

1. If you mix red and blue, you get purple.
2. If Julie has finished her homework, she may visit Jackie.
3. Laura would be sad if she hadn't made it up (make it up, *dt. sich versöhnen)* with Jonas.
4. If you have to learn your vocabulary, you needn't help me with the washing-up.
5. Sam would have bought lots of presents for Sarah's birthday if he was rich.
6. Don't disturb Dad if he's working.

a) Bedingung ist im Verlauf
b) Bedingung liegt in der Vergangenheit, die Folge in der Gegenwart
c) Verpflichtung in der Gegenwart
d) Bedingung liegt in der Gegenwart, die Folge in der Vergangenheit
e) logische Folge
f) Bedingung ist bereits erfüllt worden

Übung 2 **Überlege, welche Art von Bedingung jeweils gegeben ist und setze dann die richtige Verbform ein.**

1. Don't interrupt Mum if she .... (still, talk) on the phone.
2. If there's no battery in your personal stereo, it .... (not work).
3. Mr Parker .... (not be) angry with Sarah now if she hadn't been so lazy.
4. Steve may watch TV if he .... (already, clean) his room.
5. If Vicky's mother .... (speak, *können*) two foreign languages, she'll get the job.
6. If the Parkers had lots of money, they .... (fly) to Australia last year.

Übung 3 **Gleich hast du's geschafft! – Übersetze ins Englische.**

1. Wenn man zu viel Fastfood isst, wird man dick.

....

2. Julie wäre jetzt nicht krank, wenn sie gestern wärmere Kleidung getragen hätte.

....

....

3. Wenn du diese Sätze richtig übersetzt hast, darfst du dich Profi *(engl. pro)* nennen.

....

....

Nach dem Heraustrennen bitte hier klammern

mentor Übungsbuch

Englisch

7./8. Klasse

If-Sätze, Futurformen

Verena Rotter

Lösungsteil

(an der Perforation heraustrennen)

mentor
Eine Klasse besser.

6 7

A Futurformen
1. Will-Future für Vermutungen und Vorhersagen

Beim will-Future *kannst du im bejahten oder verneinten Satz entweder die Langform* (will / will not) *oder die Kurzform* ('ll / won't) *verwenden. Beides ist richtig.*
Der besseren Übersichtlichkeit halber findest du in der Regel im Folgenden nur eine Form.
Im mündlichen Sprachgebrauch sind Kurzformen generell üblicher.

Übung 1

Tomorrow it'll be / will be warm and sunny in South England.
There will be light winds from the South-West only.
The Midlands will be cloudy, but it will stay dry.
It will rain heavily in Scotland tomorrow.
In the Highlands there will be strong winds from the North-West and the temperature there will not go / won't go above 8°C.
In Wales it will be cloudy, but it won't rain all day.
You will even have some sunny spells in the early evening.
Beachte, dass even *zwischen dem Hilfsverb* (will) *und dem Vollverb* (have) *steht.*
In Northern Ireland it will be cloudy with lots of rain.
Temperatures won't climb above 10°C.

Übung 2

I will earn lots of money.
I will have a husband and (some) children.
I will have to cook dinner for my family.
Zur Erinnerung: have to *ist das Ersatzverb zu* must.
I won't have to be at home at 8 p.m.
I won't go to bed at 10 p.m.
My parents will be over 60.

Übung 3

1. Will I fall in love soon? / Will I soon fall in love?
2. Will I get good marks?
3. Will Petra really move away from Munich?
4. Will I get a snowboard for my birthday?

Beachte die Präposition for.
Nicht vergessen:
bekommen heißt auf Englisch get *oder* receive, *das englische* become *heißt werden!*

2. Will-Future für spontane Entschlüsse und Angebote

Übung 1

1. Sarah: "I'll do the washing-up for you, Mum."
2. Julie: "No problem, Mum, I'll go and buy some."
3. Ben & Steve: "We'll buy a new bottle for you."
4. Sarah & Steve: "We'll stay at home and we'll sit at her bedside all night, Mum."

Muttertag wird in Großbritannien übrigens im März gefeiert!

Übung 2

Das will-Future *kannst du im Deutschen entweder mit dem Futur I oder mit der Gegenwart wiedergeben.*

1. Ich verspreche (euch), dass wir um 11 Uhr / 23 Uhr zurückkommen / zurückkommen werden.
2. Ich hoffe, dass es keinen Stau gibt / geben wird.
   oder freier: ... dass wir nicht im Stau stecken (werden).
3. Ich nehme an / denke, dass Julies Temperatur / Fieber nicht weiter ansteigt / ansteigen wird.
   Nicht vergessen: der Genitiv (hier: Julies) wird im Deutschen ohne Apostroph gebildet
4. Ich rechne damit / denke / glaube, dass Julie bald einschläft / einschlafen wird.

Wenn deine Version der Übersetzung nicht genau mit den hier aufgeführten Lösungsvorschlägen übereinstimmt, heißt das nicht, dass sie falsch ist.
Zieh am besten ein Lexikon zu Rate, falls du dir nicht sicher bist.

Übung 3

1. Julie: "I'm so bored. What shall we do tonight / this evening?"
2. Sarah: "Shall I get you / fetch you a cup of tea?"
3. Steve: "Shall I turn the TV on?"
4. Sarah & Steve: "Shall we read you a story?"
5. Steve: "Shall I bring your colouring book?"

Übung 4

1. + d) Shall we go to the cinema tonight? → Vorschlag
2. + e) I wonder what the film will be like. → will-Future nach bestimmten Verben
3. + a) There will be seven billion people on our planet soon. → Vorhersage
4. + c) A: I like this sweater. – B: I'll buy it for you. → spontanes Angebot
5. + b) I think Sarah will get a good mark in her German test. → Vermutung

10 11

3. Going to-Future

Beim going to-Future *kannst du die Formen von* to be *als Langform* (am / are / is) *oder als Kurzform* ('m / 're / 's) *verwenden. Im mündlichen Sprachgebrauch sind Kurzformen üblicher.*

Übung 1

Mrs Parker: Steve, have you done the shopping yet?
Steve: Not yet, Mum. I'm going to do it later.
Mrs Parker: Sarah, have you cleaned the rooms yet?
Sarah: I've cleaned Ben and Steve's room as well as mine. But Julie's room looks such a mess. I'm not going to clean it.
Mrs Parker: I've just talked to her. She's going to clean the room herself.
Sarah: Has she got time to do it? It's her turn to scrub the kitchen floor, isn't it?
Mrs Parker: You are right, Sarah. It *is* her turn, but she isn't going to scrub the floor. She said she's still too ill …

Übung 2

1. Julie has put milk onto the stove. She forgets to turn the hot-plate off. The milk is going to boil over.
2. Steve and Eric are climbing up an old ladder to pick apples. One rung of the ladder is loose. They are going to fall off the ladder.
3. Sarah is running a bath. She leaves the bathroom and talks to her friend Vicky on the phone for an hour. The water is going to flood the whole house.
4. Ben is driving a car without a driver's licence. He hasn't slept for 24 hours. He is going to have an accident.

Übung 3

Dear Sarah,
You wrote in your last letter that you are going to give a big party together with Steve …
Where are you going to celebrate?
Who are you going to invite?
What kind of music are you going to play?
Is your mother going to make her delicious salads again?
What are you going to give Steve for his birthday?
I wish I could celebrate with you.

Yours, Laura

4. Will-Future und going to-Future im Vergleich

12 13

Übung 1

Diese Übung behandelt (feste) Pläne. Deshalb musst du hier das going to-Future *verwenden. Es bleibt dir überlassen, wie viele Sätze du mit* I, my parents, my sister / brother *(falls du Geschwister hast) oder* my friend *bildest.*
Folgende Lösungen sind nur Vorschläge!
Achte auf die richtige Form von to be.

1. I'm going to watch TV tonight.
2. My parents are going to visit my grandparents next weekend.
3. My sister is going to play tennis tonight.
4. My friend is going to visit me next weekend.
5. I'm going to read the latest novel of my favourite writer in the holidays.
6. My brother is going to learn to sail in the holidays.
7. My sister is going to give a party next weekend.

Übung 2

Bei spontanen Angeboten, wie sie in dieser Übung vorkommen, musst du das will-Future *verwenden.*

1. Sarah: "We haven't got enough biscuits."
   Vicky: "I'll bake some."
2. Steve: "We've only got fifteen CDs."
   Joe: "I'll bring my CD collection."
3. Sarah: "Oh no! I've dropped the chocolate cake!"
   Karen & Amy: "Never mind. We'll make a new one."
4. Steve: "Look! We've only got twenty glasses. We need another ten or twelve."
   Susan: "No problem. I'll go and get you twenty if you like."

Übung 3

1. Karen: "Vicky, do you think Sarah will like our present?"
   Mit think *wird eine Vermutung zum Ausdruck gebracht* → will-Future
2. Vicky: "I'm sure she'll love it."
   Nach der Wendung I'm sure *verwendet man ebenfalls das* will-Future.
3. Eric: "What are you going to give Steve?"
   Eric geht davon aus, dass Justin schon weiß, was er Steve schenken wird (und es sich nicht um eine spontane Idee handelt) → *going to-Future*
4. Justin: "I'm going to give him a poster of Andre Agassi."
   Justin hat sich schon ein Geschenk überlegt (oder bereits gekauft) → *going to-Future*
5. Justin: "I suppose Steve will put it onto the wall."
   Suppose *gehört zu den in die Zukunft weisenden Verben, nach denen das* will-Future *steht.*

14 15

5. Will-Future und going to-Future: Mixed Exercises

Übung 1

Für Vorschläge und Angebote („Soll ich …?" / „Sollen wir …?") verwendet man shall.

1. Mrs Parker: "Shall I open a window / the window / the windows?"
2. Mr Parker: "Shall I get you a chair?"
3. Mr & Mrs Parker: "Shall we go and get some more?"
4. Mr Parker: "Shall I play one of my Beatles cassettes?"
5. Mrs Parker: "Shall I drive you home?"
6. Mrs Parker: "Shall I make the guest bed for her?"

Übung 2

Grandma: Well, Steve and Sarah, what are you going to do with the money (…)?
Grandma fragt nach den Plänen, die Sarah mit dem Geld hat → going to-Future

Sarah: I've already decided that I'm going to save half of it.
Sarahs Absicht, die Hälfte zu sparen besteht schon länger → going to-Future

Grandma: And what about the other half?

Sarah: I haven't had the time to spend it yet, but I'm definitely going to buy the brand new *Spice Girls* CD.
Auch hier handelt es sich um eine feste, wohl überlegte Absicht
Beachte die Stellung von definitely!

Grandma: And what are you going to do with the rest?

Sarah: I'm going to give Mum and Dad tickets for the theatre because they helped us so much with our party.
Feste Pläne → going to-Future

Grandma: That's very nice of you, Sarah. And what are you going to do with the money, Steve?

Steve: Well, unlike Sarah, I'm certainly not going to save any of it.
Es ist Steves fester Entschluss nichts zu sparen → going to-Future
Beachte die Stellung von certainly!

Grandma: What are you going to buy then?

Steve: I haven't thought about it so far. Perhaps I'll buy a pair of new tennis shoes.
Durch perhaps *wird eine Vermutung ausgedrückt* → will-Future

Grandma: I hope I'll find nice ones.
Hope *gehört zu den Verben, die in die Zukunft weisen* → will-Future

Steve: And tomorrow I'm going to do a cycling tour with James and Eric.
Die Radtour ist bereits fest geplant → going to-Future
I'm sure I'll need some money.
Signalwort: I'm sure → will-Future

Grandma: Have you listened to the weather forecast?

Steve: Yes, I have. It will be cloudy but it won't rain.
Bei Wettervorhersagen steht das will-Future.

Übung 3

1. It will be rather cold tomorrow. → Vorhersage → will
2. Shall we go swimming? → Vorschlag → shall
3. I'm going to watch a video tonight. → Plan, feste Absicht → going to
4. I promise I'll be back in 5 minutes. → nach einem Verb, das in die Zukunft weist → will
5. Look at the sky. It's going to rain. → absehbares Ereignis → going to
6. I think Ben will pass the test easily. → Vermutung → will
7. (A: I'm too tired to do the shopping.) → Spontanes Angebot → will
B: No problem. I'll do it for you.

6. Simple Present mit zukünftiger Bedeutung

16 17

Übung 1

Steve: Excuse me, Mr Hill, when does the next bus to the city centre leave?
Mr Hill: It leaves in about ten minutes. What are you going to visit?
Eric: Well, first of all we'd like to go on a sight-seeing tour. Do you know where the tours start?
Mr Hill: They start in front of the town hall on the hour.
Steve: And I'd like to go to the *British Handcraft Museum*.
Mr Hill: You'll have to hurry then, boys. The museum closes at 4 o'clock.
Eric: And when does it open tomorrow morning? Just in case we don't manage to get there in time …
Mr Hill: I think it opens at 9 a.m. I can check that for you. Why don't you go to the inline-disco tonight?
James: Inline-disco? Great! Where does it take place and when does it begin?
Mr Hill: It's in the sports centre in Beechwood Road. And it starts at 8 p.m. and finishes at 11 p.m. But don't forget that the youth hostel closes at 10.30 p.m.

Hast du an das -s bei der 3. Person Singular (he, she, it) *gedacht?*
Nicht vergessen: nach o, s, x, z, ch *und* sh *(wie hier bei* finish*) musst du* -es *anhängen.*

Übung 2

Bei der folgenden Übung kann in der Regel der Nebensatz vor oder nach dem Hauptsatz stehen.
Beachte, dass das Verb im Hauptsatz im will-Future *und das im Nebensatz im* Simple Present *stehen muss.*

1. Steve will go to bed as soon as he returns from the cyclingtour.
   oder As soon as Steve returns from the cyclingtour, he will go to bed.
2. Sarah will take a shower before she goes to the cinema.
   oder Before Sarah goes to the cinema she will take a shower.
3. Mr Parker will phone his wife when he arrives in Birmingham.
   oder When Mr Parker arrives in Birmingham he will phone his wife.
4. The children won't start breakfast until their parents sit down at the table.

Bei der Wendung not … until *ist ein einfaches Umstellen von Haupt- und Nebensatz nicht möglich. Will man hier den Nebensatz vor den Hauptsatz stellen, hat dies eine so genannte Inversion zur Folge:*
Not until their parents arrive will the children start breakfast.
Grammatikalische Strukturen dieser Art gehören jedoch nicht zum Stoffgebiet der 7. und 8. Jahrgangsstufe.

18 19

7. Present Progressive mit zukünftiger Bedeutung

Übung 1

1. Mr Parker is going to the dentist on Wednesday.
   He is taking the car to the garage on Friday.
2. Mrs Parker is meeting her friend Liz on Saturday.
3. Ben is going to the cinema on Thursday evening.
   On Friday he is playing basketball.
4. Sarah is visiting Karen on Wednesday afternoon.
   She is going shopping on Saturday.
5. Steve is playing tennis on Tuesday and Saturday.
6. Julie is having a ballet class on Monday and an art class on Thursday.
   On Sunday she is walking Mrs Pearson's dog.

Nicht vergessen:
Bei Verlaufsformen musst du folgende Sonderformen in der Schreibweise beachten:
- *stummes* -e *entfällt:* take → he is taking
- *Konsonantenverdopplung nach kurzem, betonten Vokal:* sit → they are sitting
- -ie *wird zu* -y-: lie → she is lying

Übung 2

Julie:	Mum, Jackie has just called. She's going swimming in the afternoon. Can you drive me to the pool?
Mrs Parker:	I'm sorry, but I can't. I'm meeting Liz at 3 p.m.
Julie:	What about Dad? He surely isn't joining you and Liz, is he?
Mrs Parker:	Of course not. But he is busy, too. He's putting up new shelves in his study.
Julie:	That's too bad. But Ben could take me on his motorbike, couldn't he?
Mrs Parker:	You needn't ask him, Julie. He's just told me that he and Emma are watching videos in the afternoon. Why aren't you going by bike?
Julie:	It's got a puncture, Mum.

Übung 3

Folgende Lösungen sind wiederum nur Vorschläge.
Achte auf die Übereinstimmung zwischen dem Subjekt und der Form von to be.

1. I'm meeting a good friend this afternoon.
2. I'm going to the cinema tonight.
3. My best friend and I are playing tennis at the weekend.
4. I'm visiting my grandparents next week.

8. Gegenwartsformen mit zukünftiger Bedeutung im Vergleich

20 21

Übung 1

In dieser Übung geht es um persönlich getroffene Verabredungen bzw. Abmachungen. Deshalb ist hier das Present Progressive *(mit zukünftiger Bedeutung) zu verwenden.*

Sam: Hi, Sarah. Would you like to go to the cinema with me tonight?
Sarah: I'd love to, but I can't. I'm playing tennis with Steve at 7 p.m.
Sam: That's a pity. How about tomorrow?
Sarah: I'm sorry, but Julie and I are visiting our grandparents tomorrow evening.
Sam: What about Thursday evening then?
Sarah: I think that's not possible either. On Thursday I'm helping my parents in the garden. You know, there's so much to do in spring time. But are *you* free on Friday? Vicky and I are going to the cinema Friday night. You can join us if you like.
Sam: Of course I do …

Übung 2

Diese Übung behandelt Kinoprogramme und Busfahrpläne, also Ereignisse, die „offiziell" festgelegt sind. Die Verbformen stehen deshalb im Simple Present *(mit zukünftiger Bedeutung).*

Nicht vergessen:
Fragen und Verneinungen im Simple Present *müssen mit* do *bzw.* does *umschrieben werden.*

Sarah: Well, which film would *you* like to watch, Vicky?
Vicky: I'd like to watch *American Beauty*.
Sam: When does it start?
Vicky: It starts at 8 o'clock in the *City House* and at 10 o'clock in the *Odeon*.
Sam: And what time does the film finish?
Vicky: Well, it lasts 90 minutes, so it finishes at about 9.30 in the *City House* and at 11.30 in the *Odeon*.
Nach Zischlauten (hier: -sh) musst du in der 3. Pers. Sing. -es anhängen!
Sarah: The last bus leaves at 11.15, which means that we can't watch it in the *Odeon*. And we really have to hurry if we want to make it in time for the 8 o'clock performance. It's already 7.25.
Sam: When does the next bus leave?
Sarah: It leaves at 7.30 and it arrives at the cinema at 7.50. Well, hurry up, folks …

Übung 3

1. "Where are you going (to)?"
2. "How long are you staying?"
3. "Are you going by coach or by train?"

Die Sätze 1–3 behandeln persönlich (von der Klasse bzw. Klassleitung) gemachte Pläne
→ Present Progressive

4. "When does your train leave?"
5. "When does it arrive in Bath?"

In den Sätzen 4 und 5 geht es um Abfahrts- und Ankunftszeiten von Zügen.
→ Simple Present
Vorsicht: „er" (= der Zug) musst du mit it *übersetzen!*

6. "Where are you staying?"

Die Entscheidung, wo Sarahs Klasse übernachtet, ist wiederum persönlicher Art
→ Present Progressive

22 23

9. Future Progressive

Übung 1

	true	false
1. Mr Parker will be having lunch at 2.30 p.m.	○	⊗
2. Mr Parker will be discussing the new project at 11.30 a.m.	⊗	○
3. Mr Parker will be meeting the new team assistant at 9 a.m.	○	⊗
4. Mr Parker will be seeing Mr Jackson before lunch.	○	⊗
5. Mr Parker will be having a sales talk in the afternoon.	⊗	○

Übung 2

Beim Future Progressive *kannst du ebenso wie beim* will-Future *in der Regel zwischen Langform* (will / will not) *und Kurzform* ('ll / won't) *wählen.*
Wie bei allen Verlaufsformen musst du auch beim Future Progressive *die Sonderformen in der Schreibweise berücksichtigen (s. Lösungskapitel 7).*

Next week …

1. … I'll be sleeping in a youth hostel.
2. … Mum won't be preparing breakfast for me.
3. … Vicky, Karen and I will be having breakfast together.
4. … we'll be visiting the famous Roman baths.
5. … I'll be sending a postcard to Laura from Bath.
6. … Sam and Daniel will be living on cheeseburgers.
7. … Steve won't be playing tennis.
8. … I'll be talking to Vicky for hours.
9. … I won't be sleeping at 10.30 p.m.
10. … Steve and I will be missing our parents.

Übung 3

1. What will you be doing tonight / this evening?
2. Will you be watching the tennis match tomorrow?
   Die Wendung "sich etwas anschauen" (→ watch sth.) *ist im Englischen nicht reflexiv!*
3. Will you be using your dictionary next week?
   Eine derartige Formulierung kann (muss aber nicht!) auf höfliche Art und Weise auf die Frage vorbereiten, ob du dir das Lexikon ausleihen könntest.
4. When will you be leaving the house this afternoon?
5. Will you be returning before 11 o'clock?
6. When will you be having dinner today?

Beachte, dass das Future Progressive *im Deutschen mit der Gegenwart (→ Was machst du heute Abend?) oder mit dem Futur I (→ Wirst du dir morgen das Tennisspiel anschauen?) wiedergegeben werden kann.*

10. Future Perfect

24 25

Übung 1

1. Next month Mr Parker will have worked about two thousand days in this company.
2. He will have spent about three thousand hours on trains, buses and planes.
3. He will have talked to more than a thousand different customers.
4. He will have developed more than eighty computer programmes.
   Beachte, dass bei developed *der Endkonsonant* (-p) *nicht verdoppelt wird. Der vorangehende Vokal* (-o-) *ist zwar kurz, aber nicht betont. Die Betonung liegt auf der zweiten Silbe* (-ve-).
5. He will have given about 250 lectures.
6. He will have travelled (→ *British English*) / will have traveled (→ *American English*) to forty European cities.

Sicher hast du gemerkt, dass du beim Future Perfect *in der Bildung der 3. Form fit sein musst.*
Hier eine kleine Wiederholung:

regelmäßige Verben	
• *Grundform* + -ed:	work → will have worked
Sonderformen in der Schreibweise	
• *stummes* -e *entfällt:*	prepare → will have prepared
• *Konsonantenverdopplung nach kurzem, betonten Vokal:*	stop → will have stopped
• -y *nach Konsonant wird zu* -i-:	carry → will have carried
unregelmäßige Verben	
Hier hilft nur eins: auswendig lernen!	

Übung 2

1. Will Mr and Mrs Parker have painted the front door by 11 o'clock? –
   Yes, they will have painted it by 11 o'clock.
2. Will they have taken the curtains down by 3 o'clock? –
   No, they won't have taken them down until 4 o'clock.
3. Will Ben and Steve have vacuumed the carpets by 12 o'clock? –
   Yes, they will have vacuumed them by 12 o'clock.
4. Will they have scrubbed the floors by 12 o'clock? –
   No, they won't have scrubbed them until 1 o'clock.
   Hast du an die Konsonantenverdopplung gedacht?
5. Will Sarah and Julie have cleaned the cupboards by 12 o'clock? –
   No, they won't have cleaned them until 1 o'clock.
6. Will they have dusted the furniture by 6 o'clock ? –
   Yes, they will have dusted it by 6 o'clock.

Beachte, dass furniture *im Englischen im Singular steht (im Gegensatz zur deutschen Übersetzung: die Möbel). Das zugehörige Personalpronomen ist deshalb* it.

Übung 3

1. The Parkers will have finished spring-cleaning by 4 p.m.
2. Next month the Parkers will have lived here for 20 / twenty years.
   oder The Parkers will have lived here for 20 / twenty years next month.

Nicht vergessen:
Im Englischen steht die Ortsangabe (here) *vor der Zeitangabe* (for twenty years).

3. Will Mr Parker have left the house by 8 o'clock?

26 27

11. Futurformen im Überblick

Übung 1

buy	going to-Future	(bejaht) (Frage)	I'm going to buy are you going to buy?
do	Future Perfect	(bejaht) (verneint)	he will have done we won't have done
arrive	Simple Present	(Frage) (verneint)	does it arrive? it doesn't arrive *Hast du an die Umschreibung gedacht?*
lie	Future Progressive	(bejaht) (Frage)	she will be lying will they be lying? *Nicht vergessen: -ie- wird hier zu -y-!*
rain	will-Future	(Frage) (verneint)	will it rain? it won't rain
stay	Present Progressive	(bejaht) (Frage)	I'm staying is he staying?

Übung 2

1. Beim Stadtbummel: „Das ist ja ein tolles T-Shirt! Das kauf' ich mir!"
   Futurform im Englischen: will-Future
   Begründung: spontaner Entschluss
2. Am Bahnschalter: „Wann fährt der nächste Zug nach Köln?"
   Futurform im Englischen: Simple Present
   Begründung: zukünftiges Ereignis, das durch einen Fahrplan festgelegt ist
3. Du träumst abends im Bett vor dich hin: „Morgen um diese Zeit sitze ich im Zug."
   Futurform im Englischen: Future Progressive
   Begründung: Handlung, die zu einem bestimmten Zeitpunkt in der Zukunft abläuft
4. Du schaukelst in der Schule ganz wild auf deinem Stuhl.
   Dein Lehrer meint: „Du wirst gleich runterfallen!"
   Futurform im Englischen: going to-Future
   Begründung: absehbares Ereignis (für das es Anzeichen gibt)
5. Du bringst dein kaputtes Fahrrad zum Reparieren und fragst:
   „Wann werden Sie das Rad repariert haben?"
   Futurform im Englischen: Future Perfect
   Begründung: Ereignis, das (zu einem bestimmten Zeitpunkt) in der Zukunft bereits abgeschlossen sein wird
6. Eine Freundin möchte wissen, was du morgen machst.
   Du sagst: „Meine Cousine kommt morgen."
   Futurform im Englischen: Present Progressive
   Begründung: Verabredung (in der nahen Zukunft)

12. Abschlusstest Futurformen

28 29

Übung 1

1. At 8.45 a.m. Steve and Sarah will have left Reading. They will be sitting in the train to Bath.
2. At 10.15 they will have arrived in Bath.
3. At 10.30 the allocation of the rooms will be taking place.
4. At 12 o'clock everybody will be having lunch.
5. At 1.30 p.m. they will be playing volleyball.
6. By 2.45 the class will have gone to the city centre.
7. At 3.30 they will be visiting the Roman baths.
8. At 4 o'clock they will be having a coffee break.
9. At 5 o'clock everybody will be looking at the beautiful art objects (…)
10. By 6.30 the class will have returned to the youth hostel.

Übung 2

Signalwörter sind unterstrichen!

Steve: What are we going to do / are we doing tomorrow?
feste Pläne in der nahen Zukunft → going to-Future *oder* Pres. Progressive*

Mr Jackson: Well, tomorrow we are going on a sight-seeing tour first.
Bei to go *verwendet man für Pläne das* Present Progressive!

Emily: When does it start?

Mr Jackson: The tour starts at 9 o'clock. Our bus leaves from in front of the youth hostel at half past eight and arrives at the town hall at eight-fifty.
Die Stadtbesichtigung ist durch ein Programm festgelegt → Simple Present

Jenny: What do we have to take with us?

Mrs Leech: I think you'll need an umbrella. I've just listened to the weather forecast. Tomorrow it will be cloudy with some showers of rain.
Wettervorhersage → will-Future

Jenny: Oh no! I have forgotten my umbrella!

Sarah: No problem. I'll lend you one. (…) → *spontanes Angebot*

Sam: When does the tour finish?

Mr Jackson: It finishes at 11.30 a.m.

Donna: What are we going to do afterwards?

Mrs Leech: If you want to, you can spend the lunch-break together in groups (…)

Daniel: Great! Shall we have lunch at McDonald's?

Sam: Good idea, Daniel! Are you going to eat seven cheeseburgers again?
Absicht / Vorsatz → going to-future

Daniel: If I have enough time, I will be able to eat eight or more.
Bedingungssatz Typ I → *im Hauptsatz:* will-Future

Mr Jackson: But don't forget to be back at the town hall at 1 p.m.

Sam: We promise we'll be back on time. → will-Future *nach bestimmten Verben*
By this time Daniel will surely have finished his eighth cheeseburger.
Sarah, what are you doing / will you be doing / are you going to do at lunch time? → *Pläne für einen bestimmten Zeitpunkt in der Zukunft*

Sarah: Well, Vicky and I have decided to spend the lunch-break at the river. At 12 o'clock we will be sitting on a bench in the sunshine.

Sam: But there won't be any sunshine tomorrow … → *Wetterbericht*

Sarah: That's a pity. But I think Vicky and I will have a nice break all the same. Without loads of cheeseburgers!

> * *Statt des* going to-Future *kannst du das* Present Progressive *nur dann verwenden, wenn der Satz eine Zeitangabe enthält, die verdeutlicht, dass das Ereignis in der Zukunft stattfindet.*

B If-Sätze
1. Grundlagen

Übung 1

1. Mr Parker / win / in the lottery	he / buy / a car / for Ben
Bedingung	Folge
2. Sarah / go / to Sam's party	he / invite / her
Folge	Bedingung
3. Mrs Parker / be / happy	Julie / help / her / with the housework
Folge	Bedingung
4. Steve / work / harder	he / get / a good mark
Bedingung	Folge
5. Julie and Jackie / not go / to the zoo	it / rain / tomorrow
Folge	Bedingung
6. The Parkers / go on holiday / to Spain	they / have / enough money
Folge	Bedingung

Übung 2

1. If Mr Parker hurries, he'll catch the train.
2. If I were you, I would work harder.
3. We can go outside if it stops raining.
4. Can you answer the phone if it rings?
5. If Daniel hadn't eaten eight cheeseburgers, he wouldn't have been sick afterwards.
6. Sarah would buy this skirt if it wasn't pink.
7. If you ever go to New York, you must visit the *Museum of Modern Art.*
8. Ben would be really unhappy if he didn't pass his driving-test.

> *Nicht vergessen:*
> *Ein Komma wird nur gesetzt, wenn der Nebensatz* (if-clause) *vor dem Hauptsatz steht.*

Übung 3

1. Sarah will take a hot shower when she returns from Bath.
   „Wenn" hat in diesem Satz die Bedeutung von „sobald". Würde man hier if *einsetzen, hieße das, dass es nicht sicher ist, ob Sarah überhaupt aus Bath zurückkommt!*
2. Laura will get the postcard next Wednesday if Sarah posts it on Friday.
   Hier handelt es sich um eine Bedingung: Laura wird die Karte am Mittwoch bekommen unter der Voraussetzung, dass Sarah sie am Freitag einwirft.
3. If Steve were as old as Ben, he could take driving-lessons, too.
   Ben ist und bleibt älter als Steve; der Satz handelt also von einer unmöglichen Bedingung.
4. Ben: "I need more pocket money, Dad ..."
   Mr Parker: "You'll get five pounds if you mow the lawn."
   Ben wird die fünf Pfund nur bekommen, falls er den Rasen mäht (→ Bedingung).
   Ben: "O.K., I'll do it when I've finished my homework."
   Ben gibt hier einen Zeitpunkt an: sobald er mit den Hausaufgaben fertig ist, wird er den Rasen mähen.

> *Tipp:*
> *Falls du dir bei einer solchen Einsetzübung nicht sicher bist, machst du am besten immer die Gegenprobe und versuchst das Wörtchen „wenn" durch „falls" bzw. „sobald" zu ersetzen.*

2. Typ I mit will-Future

32 33

Übung 1

1. + e) If Steve doesn't hurry, he'll miss the bus.
2. + f) If you read through the text carefully, you'll be able to answer the questions easily.
3. + g) Tom will join us at the cinema if you don't mind.
4. + b) My mother will be angry with me if I don't help her with the housework.
5. + a) If you help me with the maths homework, I'll help you with the French translation.
6. + d) I will return this book to Sue if I see her today.
7. + c) If you bring some sandwiches, I'll bring some cans of lemonade.

Übung 2

Sam: Hi, Sarah. What are you doing at the weekend?
Sarah: If the weather is nice, Vicky and I will go shopping on Saturday.
Sam: And what will you do if the weather isn't nice?
Sarah: We will probably not stay at home even if it isn't sunny.
Beachte, dass probably *nach dem Hilfsverb* (will) *steht.*
But if it rains, Vicky and I will meet at my place and we'll prepare our geography paper together.
Sam: Do you need some help?
Sarah: If you are keen on that stuff, we won't send you away.
Sam: What are you doing on Saturday evening? There's a good film at the *Odeon*.
Sarah: Well, my parents are spending a day in London on Saturday. And Julie mustn't be left alone. But if they return in time, I will be able to join you.
Sam: And if they don't come back in time?
Sarah: Hm ... I've got an idea! If my parents don't return in time, we will watch some videos. Is that okay with you?
Sam: Great! See you tomorrow ...

Übung 3

Folgende Lösungen sind natürlich wieder nur Vorschläge!
Achte darauf, dass der if-*Satz im* Simple Present *und der Hauptsatz im* will-Future *steht.*

1. If the weather is nice tomorrow, I will go shopping.
2. If it doesn't rain this afternoon, I'll give a garden party.
   Hast du an die Umschreibung mit does *gedacht?*
3. If my friend (Tom / Steffi / ...) visits me on Saturday, we'll go to the cinema.
   Achtung: my friend = he / she → *das -s beim Verb nicht vergessen!*
4. If my parents give me more pocket money next month, I'll buy some comics / a hamster.

34 35

3. Typ I mit Imperativ oder modalem Hilfsverb

Übung 1

1. + f) If the water is too cold, we can't swim in the lake.
2. + h) Julie must put on some weight if she weighs less than 20 kilos.
3. + b) Steve can win the tennis trophy if he is in good form tomorrow.
4. + g) If we don't hurry, we won't see the beginning of the film.
5. + d) If you help me with the washing-up today, you needn't help me tomorrow.
6. + e) You must do your homework on Sunday if you don't do it on Friday or Saturday.
7. + a) If a stranger wants you to open the door, you mustn't let him in.
8. + c) Sarah can go to the cinema with Sam if Mr and Mrs Parker return in time.

Übung 2

1. If you go to* Paris, you can see the *Eiffel Tower*.
2. If you visit Vienna, you must go to* the *Hofburg*.
3. If you go to London, you must have a look at *St Paul's Cathedral*.
4. If you visit Berlin, you can walk along the *Ku'damm*.
5. If you go to Florence, you must visit the *Uffizien*.

* go to *kann im Deutschen sowohl „fahren nach" bedeuten als auch „gehen zu" (im Sinne von „besichtigen")*

Übung 3

1. If Julie gets a good mark in the maths test, she may go to the zoo.
2. If Sarah doesn't come back on time today, she mustn't go out tomorrow.
   Nicht vergessen: „nicht dürfen" heißt auf Englisch must not
3. If Steve isn't back at 8 o'clock, he can't / cannot watch the film.
4. If Ben wants more pocket money, he must help his father in the garden.
5. If the Parkers take on a housekeeper, Mrs Parker needn't do all the housework alone anymore.

Vergleiche die Wortstellung:

Wenn Ben mehr Taschengeld will, *<u>muss er</u> seinem Vater im Garten <u>helfen</u>.* → *Im Deutschen steht das modale Hilfsverb vor dem Subjekt; das Vollverb rückt an das Satzende.*	If Ben wants more pocket money, <u>he must help</u> his father in the garden. → *Im Englischen dagegen gilt die Reihenfolge Subjekt + Hilfsverb + Vollverb.*

Übung 4

1. Vergiss nicht deinen (Regen-)Schirm, wenn / falls es regnet.
   oder Vergiss deinen Schirm nicht, …
2. Räum dein Zimmer auf, wenn du deine Sachen / dein Zeugs nicht findest.
3. Hilf mir bei der Hausarbeit, wenn du nichts Besseres zu tun hast.

4. Typ I: Mixed Exercise

36 37

Übung 1

Dear Sarah,
Have you already decided when to come?
If you come in August, the weather will surely be nice.
Beachte die Stellung von surely.
If you're / you are interested in the sights of Munich, we can go on a sight-seeingtour.
But we needn't do one if you think that's boring.
If you like going for walks, we must go to the *Englischer Garten*.
If you want to buy clothes in Munich, I will show you some fantastic shops.
I'm sure that we'll have a great time together.
Write soon. Love, Laura

Übungsvariante für Fortgeschrittene:
Decke im Übungsteil die rechte Spalte ab und versuche den gesamten Brief ins Englische zu übersetzen.

Übung 2

1. If I see her tomorrow, I will ask her whether she's got any plans for the weekend.
2. If she doesn't have / hasn't got any plans, I will suggest that we go on a cycling tour.
3. If she hasn't got / doesn't have a bike, she can borrow my sister's bike.
   In den Sätzen 2) und 3) kannst du im if*-Satz entweder* doesn't have *oder* hasn't got *verwenden.*
4. If she doesn't like cycling, I will ask her to go to the cinema with me.
5. If she wants to go to the cinema, she may choose a film she would like to see.
6. If she chooses a film I've already seen, I won't tell her.
7. If she really goes to the cinema with me, I will be extremely happy.

Übung 3

Auch diese Lösungen stellen wieder nur Vorschläge dar!

1. I'll be very happy if I get a new bike for my birthday / for Christmas.
2. If I get a good mark in my next English test, my parents will give me some extra pocket money.
3. If my sister / brother uses my computer without asking me, she / he mustn't go into my room again.
4. I'll get very angry if I find out that my friend has lied to me.
5. If it rains tomorrow, I can't play tennis.
6. I'll be thankful if my grandma gets better soon.

38 | 39

5. Typ II mit unwahrscheinlicher Bedingung

Übung 1

Im Hauptsatz kannst du hier, wenn dies Sinn ergibt, zwischen den Hilfsverben would, could *und* might *variieren. Beachte aber den Bedeutungsunterschied (→ würde / könnte / würde vielleicht) und überlege, was am besten passt.*

1. If Sarah cleaned her room more often, it wouldn't look such a mess.
   Hier erscheint would *am sinnvollsten.*
2. Ben would get more pocket money if he helped his father more often in the garden.
   Auch hier passt would *am besten, denkbar wären aber auch* could *(→ er könnte mehr bekommen; es liegt also in seiner Macht) oder* might *(→ er würde vielleicht mehr bekommen, sicher ist es jedoch nicht).*
3. If Steve practised even harder, he could / would / might become the best tennis player in his school.
4. Julie would have more time for painting pictures if she didn't take so many ballet classes.
   Would *ist hier wohl die beste Lösung, denkbar (mit Bedeutungsunterschied!) sind aber auch* could *und* might.
   Hast du an die Umschreibung mit did *gedacht?*

Übung 2

1. If Ben found a snake in his bed, he would kill it.
2. If Sarah found a snake in her bed, she would call the police.
3. If Steve found a snake in his bed, he would catch it.
4. If Julie found a snake in her bed, she would scream.
5. If Ben met an alien, he would say "hello".
6. If Sarah met an alien, she would ask its name.
7. If Steve met an alien, he wouldn't do anything.
8. If Julie met an alien, she would be afraid.

Schon gemerkt? – Zur Bildung von Verbformen im Simple Past *musst du fit in den unregelmäßigen Verben sein. Wie wär's mit einer gelegentlichen Wiederholung?*
Zur Erinnerung:

> *Bei regelmäßigen Verben werden die 2. und die 3. Form des Verbs wie folgt gebildet:*
> - *Grundform* + -ed
> - *Die „Sonderformen in der Schreibweise", die bei regelmäßigen Verben für die 2. und die 3. Form gleichermaßen zutreffen, findest du im Lösungskapitel 10.*

Übung 3

1. If I found a snake in my bed, I would run away and scream.
   Wenn ich eine Schlange in meinen Bett fände / finden würde*, würde ich weglaufen und schreien.
2. If I met an alien, I would talk to him.
   Wenn ich einen Außerirdischen träfe / treffen würde*, würde ich mich mit ihm unterhalten.

> * *Im Deutschen kannst du neben dem korrekten Konjunktiv (→ fände / träfe) auch die umgangssprachlichen Formen (→ finden würde / treffen würde) verwenden.*
> *Vorsicht ist bei einer Übersetzung vom Deutschen ins Englische geboten:*
> *Im Englischen darf im* if-*Satz kein* would *stehen!!!*

6. Typ II mit unmöglicher Bedingung

40 41

Bedingungssätze dieser Art verwendet man, wie in den Übungen 1, 2 und 4, z. B. für Tagträume und Wunschdenken.

Übung 1

1. If I had dark hair, I would look much better.
2. If I didn't have such short legs, I could wear mini-skirts.
   Durch could *wird hier stärker die Möglichkeit (→ könnte) betont;* would *ist aber auch möglich.*
3. I would be much happier if my hair wasn't / weren't* so curly.
4. If I was / were* taller, I could wear these fashionable trousers.
   Auch bei diesem Satz sind could *oder* would *verwendbar.*
5. I wouldn't be so self-conscious if I didn't have so many spots.

> * *In den Bedingungssätzen vom Typ II kann statt* was *(der für* I, he, she *und* it *üblichen Form von* to be) *auch* were *(vgl. dt. „wäre") verwendet werden.*
> *In der Wendung* "If I were you ..." *steht jedoch immer* were.

Übung 2

1. If I knew Lucy's number, I would phone her.
2. If she wasn't / weren't so beautiful, I would dare to tell her (that) I love her.
3. If she was / were my girl-friend, I would be the happiest person in the world.
4. If I had lots of money, I would buy her anything she wants.

Übung 3

1. You: "If I were you, I would go / 'd go to the hairdresser's."
2. You: "If I were you, I would tell her the truth."
3. You: "If I were you, I would do a lot of sport."
4. You: "If I were you, I wouldn't buy them."

Übung 4

Wie üblich bei derartigen Übungen, sollen die folgenden Lösungen nur Vorschläge darstellen und dir als Orientierung dienen.

1. If I were eighteen, I wouldn't have to be at home at 9 p.m.
   Wenn ich 18 wäre, müsste ich nicht um 9 Uhr abends zu Hause sein.
2. If I were a pop star, I would be rich and famous / would have fans all over the world.
   Wenn ich ein Popstar wäre, wäre ich reich und berühmt / hätte ich auf der ganzen Welt Fans.
3. If I had lots of money, I would give parties every weekend.
   Wenn ich viel Geld hätte, würde ich jedes Wochenende Partys geben.

Beachte, dass die in diesem Satztyp häufig vorkommenden Verben „hätte" und „wäre" im Englischen unterschiedliche Entsprechungen haben, je nachdem, ob sie im if-Satz oder im Hauptsatz stehen. Vergleiche:

***if*-Satz**	***Hauptsatz***
Wenn ich ein Popstar wäre,	*wäre ich reich und berühmt.*
→ If I were a pop star,	→ I would be rich and famous.
Wenn ich viel Geld hätte, ...	*... hätte ich auf der ganzen Welt Fans.*
→ If I had lots of money, ...	→ ... I would have fans all over the world.

Um Fehler zu vermeiden, solltest du – insbesondere bei deutsch-englischen Übersetzungen – genau überprüfen, ob das Verb im Haupt- oder im Nebensatz (if-Satz) steht.

42 : 43

7. Typ I und Typ II im Vergleich

Übung 1

Typ I	Typ II
a) Steve and Eric can play tennis if the sun comes out later. c) If the sun shines, we won't stay indoors. f) Tidy up your room if you don't know what else to do.	b) If I were you, I wouldn't tell her secrets any more. d) What would you do if you met the Queen in the street? e) If Ben had enough time today, he could help his father in the garden.

Übung 2

1. If my grandma gives me some money, I can buy a new skateboard.
   can buy = *modales Hilfsverb im Hauptsatz → Typ I; hast du bei* give *an das -s gedacht?*
2. Sarah would / could / might phone Laura more often if it was cheaper.
   was = Simple Past *im* if-*Satz → Typ II*
3. If you help me with the washing-up, I will clean your shoes.
   help = Simple Present *im* if-*Satz → Typ I*
4. If I were you, I would tell my parents the truth.
   would tell = Conditional I *im Hauptsatz → Typ II*
   Nicht vergessen: In dieser Wendung kannst du nur were *verwenden.*
5. Would you mind if I opened the window?
   would … mind = Conditional I *im Hauptsatz → Typ II*
6. Go to your room if you keep on shouting like this.
   keep on = Simple Present im if-Satz → Typ I
   Da kein Subjekt angegeben ist, muss hier ein Imperativ gebildet werden.

Übung 3

1. a) If Eric were / was here now, we could play tennis.
   Tatsache ist, dass Steve allein ist → unmögliche Bedingung (Typ II)
   Statt could *kannst du auch* would *oder* might *einsetzen.*
   b) If he comes later, we will play / can play tennis.
   Es ist möglich, dass Eric später noch kommt → Typ I
2. a) "I would love to buy this dress if it was / were red."
   Das Kleid ist aber blau → unmögliche Bedingung (Typ II)
   b) "If I find a red one in another shop, I'll buy it."
   Die Möglichkeit, ein rotes zu finden, besteht noch → Typ I
3. a) We will go inside if it gets colder later.
   Es ist durchaus möglich, dass es später kälter wird → Typ I
   b) If it weren't / wasn't sunny, we wouldn't spend the day in the garden.
   Tatsache ist aber, dass es im Moment sonnig ist → unmögliche Bedingung (Typ II)
4. a) If Julie didn't take her doll to school, they wouldn't call her "little baby".
   Noch nimmt sie ihre Puppe mit in die Schule → unmögliche (weil den Tatsachen widersprechende) Bedingung (Typ II)
   b) If she leaves it at home next week, they won't laugh at her.
   Es ist aber möglich, dass sie sie nächste Woche zu Hause läßt (weil sie von den Hänseleien genug hat) → Typ I

8. Typ III

44 45

Übung 1

1. If Ben had had enough time, he'd have helped = would have helped his father in the garden.
2. Sarah wouldn't have gone to the cinema if she'd known = had known that it was such a bad film.
3. If he'd felt = had felt better, Steve would have won the tennis match.
4. We'd have gone = would have gone to the theatre if we'd had = had had enough money.

Alles klar?

> *Bei den Bedingungssätzen vom Typ III steht die Kurzform* 'd
> - *für* had *im* if-*Satz und*
> - *für* would *im Hauptsatz*

Übung 2

Mrs Parker: Hi, Steve. How was the match?
Steve: It was awful, Mum. I lost.
Mrs Parker: Never mind, Steve. But what happened?
Steve: It was just too hot. If it hadn't been so hot, I'd have won / would have won the match.
Mrs Parker: Why is that?
Steve: My hands were wet with sweat. If I hadn't sweated so much, I'd have hit more balls.
Mrs Parker: Did you have enough mineral water with you?
Steve: No, just one bottle. If I'd taken / had taken more water with me, I wouldn't have got tired so quickly.
And to make things worse I even forgot my sunglasses.
I'm sure I would have played much better if I hadn't forgotten my sunglasses.
Mrs Parker: Don't blame it on the sunglasses, Steve. You just had a bad day.
Steve: You're probably right, Mum. If I had been in form, I wouldn't have lost the match.

Vergleiche:

Hauptsatz	**if-*Satz***
I'm sure I would have played much better → *Ich bin (mir) sicher, dass ich viel besser gespielt hätte,*	if I hadn't forgotten my sunglasses. → *wenn ich meine Sonnenbrille nicht vergessen hätte.*

→ *Während hier im Deutschen beide Verbformen mit „hätte" gebildet werden, steht im Englischen dafür* would have … *im Hauptsatz und* had(n't) … *im* if-*Satz.*
Daran solltest du insbesondere bei Übersetzungen vom Deutschen ins Englische denken! Beachte auch, dass die Verbformen in Bedingungssätzen vom Typ III – je nach Verb – einmal mit „hätte …" (→ I would have played / I hadn't forgotten*) und einmal mit „wäre …"* (I wouldn't have got / I had been) *zu übersetzen sind.*

Übung 3

1. If I had gone to bed earlier, I wouldn't have overslept.
2. I wouldn't have been hungry all morning if I had had time for breakfast.
3. If I had studied enough for the maths test, I could have answered all the questions.
oder I could have answered all the questions if I had studied enough for the maths test.

46 | 47

9. Unmögliche Bedingungen im Vergleich (Typ II und Typ III)

Übung 1

1. If Sam had enough money, he'd buy a bunch of flowers for Sarah.
   Im if-*Satz steht* Simple Past → *Typ II (Bezug auf die Gegenwart)*
2. If Sam had had enough money last week, he would have bought a bottle of perfume for Sarah.
   Im if-*Satz steht* Past Perfect → *Typ III (Bezug auf die Vergangenheit)*
3. Ben would be sad if Emma wasn't / weren't here now.
   Im Hauptsatz steht Conditional I → *Typ II*
4. Ben would have been sad if he hadn't passed his driving-test.
   Im Hauptsatz steht Conditional II → *Typ III*
5. Julie would have painted some pictures if it had rained yesterday.
   Im if-*Satz steht* Past Perfect → *Typ III*
6. Julie wouldn't sit in the garden if it was raining now.
   Im if-*Satz steht* Simple Past → *Typ II*

Übung 2

1. If Julie found her pencil, she could draw now.
2. Steve would have played tennis yesterday if his right leg hadn't hurt.
3. If Ben didn't have such a lot of homework to do, he would / could see Emma more often these days.
   oder Ben would / could see Emma more often these days if he didn't have (...)
4. Sarah could / would have baked a cake last Sunday if she hadn't forgotten to buy some eggs.
   oder If Sarah hadn't forgotten to buy some eggs, she could / would have baked (...)

Übung 3

> *Achte beim Übersetzen darauf, dass du die „Feinabstimmungen" der Bedingungssätze* (→ would / could / might) *ins Englische übernimmst!*

If I hadn't been at home yesterday, he couldn't have visited me.
If we hadn't met, we wouldn't have argued.
He might not have gone if I had listened to him.
Bis zu dieser Stelle beziehen sich die Sätze auf die Vergangenheit (→ Signalwort: yesterday*). Da das Gewesene nicht mehr geändert, also die Bedingung jeweils nicht mehr erfüllt werden kann, müssen hier Bedingungssätze vom Typ III stehen.*
I'm extremely unhappy now.
What would you do if you were me?
I would be so happy if he were / was here now.
Die letzten beiden Sätze des Briefes beziehen sich auf die Gegenwart (→ Signalwort: now*). Es handelt sich in beiden Fällen um Bedingungen, die unmöglich sind, weil sie den gegebenen Tatsachen widersprechen (Sarah kann nicht Laura sein und Jonas ist nicht hier!), deshalb musst du hier den Typ II verwenden.*
*Hast du daran gedacht, dass im Englischen kein Komma gesetzt wird, wenn der Hauptsatz vor dem Nebensatz (*if*-Satz) steht?*

10. Typ I, Typ II und Typ III im Vergleich

48 | 49

Übung 1

1. If Julie found a purse in the street, she'd take it to the police. → Typ II
2. Mr Parker will miss the train if he doesn't hurry. → Typ I
3. Steve might have won the match if he had been in form. → Typ III
4. If Ben has got enough money, he'll give a big party next week. → Typ I
5. If Sarah hadn't forgotten her textbook at school, she would have been able to do her homework. → Typ III

Übung 2

1. Wenn Sarah gestern zu Hause gewesen wäre, hätte Sam sie ins Kino eingeladen.
   zeitl. Bezug: Vergangenheit   Bedingung: nicht mehr erfüllbar   Typ III
   Übersetzung:
   If Sarah had been at home yesterday, Sam would have invited her to the cinema.
2. *Der Wetterbericht hat für morgen schönes Wetter und Temperaturen bis zu 27°C vorhergesagt.*
   Wenn es morgen regnen würde, könnten Sarah und Sam kein Picknick machen.
   zeitl. Bezug: Zukunft   Bedingung: unwahrscheinlich   Typ II
   Übersetzung:
   If it rained tomorrow, Sarah and Sam couldn't have a picnic.
3. Sarah wird ihre neuen Shorts anziehen, falls es morgen richtig heiß wird.
   zeitl. Bezug: Zukunft   Bedingung: wahrscheinlich   Typ I
   Übersetzung:
   Sarah will wear her new shorts if it gets really hot tomorrow.
4. Wenn Sam gerne schwimmt, kann er ein Bad im See nehmen.
   zeitl. Bezug: Gegenwart   Bedingung: erfüllt   Typ I
   Übersetzung:
   If Sam likes swimming, he can have a swim in the lake.
   Nicht vergessen:
   – *der See heißt* "the lake"
   – *die See (= das Meer) heißt* "the sea"
5. *Bevor Sam und Sarah am nächsten Tag losziehen, sagt Mrs Parker zu Sarah:*
   „Ich an deiner Stelle (= Wenn ich du wäre) würde (ich) ein Insektenschutzmittel mitnehmen."
   zeitl. Bezug: Gegenwart   Bedingung: unmöglich   Typ II
   Übersetzung:
   "If I were you, I would take an insect repellent with me."
   Hast du daran gedacht, dass vor einem nachfolgenden Vokal (hier i-*) der unbestimmte Artikel „*an*" lauten muss?*

50 51

11. Abschlusstest if-Sätze

Übung 1

1. Ben wouldn't go to school by motorbike if it rained tomorrow. → es ist unwahrscheinlich, dass es regnet
2. If Jenny comes to Ben's party, she'll bring a chocolate cake. → mit Jennys Kommen ist zu rechnen
3. Sarah wouldn't have got a bad mark if she had worked harder. → Sarah hat zu wenig für die Schule getan
4. If Vicky had known that Sarah was at home, she would have visited her. → Vicky wusste nicht, dass Sarah zu Hause ist
5. Mr Parker could drive Julie to the pool if he was back at 4 p.m. → er wird um 16 Uhr wohl nicht zurück sein

Übung 2

Sarah: Hi, Laura. How are you?
Laura: Hi, Sarah. Not too good. Are you in a hurry?
Sarah: Of course I'm not. I wouldn't phone you if I didn't have time. Why are you asking?
Sarah hat Zeit, also widerspricht die Bedingung den gegebenen Tatsachen → Typ II
Laura: Well, it's quite a long story … Jonas and I had another argument.
Sarah: Oh dear! What happened?
Laura: I was playing games on Jonas' computer when it suddenly crashed. I really felt sorry. If it hadn't been me who was playing, it wouldn't have been my fault.
Sarah: I don't think that's such a big problem. What did Jonas do then?
Laura: He called me a fool. Then I went mad and threw some CDs at him. You know, I wouldn't have thrown CDs at him if he hadn't called me a fool.
Sarah: Did they hit him?
Laura: No, the CDs missed him (…). I think I'd have felt sorry if I had hurt him.
Hier handelt es sich um drei rein theoretische Annahmen in Bezug auf die Vergangenheit (if it hadn't been … / if he hadn't called me … / if I had hurt …) *→ Typ III*
Sarah: What did you do then?
Laura: I left at once. And Jonas didn't stop me going.
Sarah: Have you heard anything from him since?
Laura: No, not yet. And I'm sure that he won't phone me. If he phoned and said he was sorry that he'd called me a fool, everything would be all right again. But I think it's over.
Diese Bedingungen (phone / say) *beziehen sich auf die Zukunft. Da sie aber unwahrscheinlich sind* (… I'm sure that he won't phone me) *wird Typ II verwendet.*
What would you do if you were me?
Sarah: Well, I think it's not just his fault. If I were you, I would call him and ask him (…)
Sarah kann nicht Laura sein → unmögliche Bedingung in der Gegenwart → Typ II
Laura: Maybe you're right, Sarah. If he doesn't call me within the next few hours, I will call him. *→ wahrscheinliche Bedingung → Typ I*
Just a second, Sarah. The door bell is ringing. If it is Jonas, I'll tell him that I'm really sorry and that I still love him …

Übung 3

Ich habe eine 4 in der Matheschulaufgabe. Iii! Wenn ich mehr getan / härter gearbeitet hätte, hätte ich nicht so eine / keine solche schlechte Note bekommen. Und vielleicht hätte ich besser abgeschnitten, wenn Mr Summer den Stoff richtig / anständig erklärt hätte. Sam sagte / hat gesagt: "Ich an deiner Stelle würde mir keine Sorgen machen. Du hast genügend gute Noten." Vielleicht hat er Recht. Wenn ich nicht nochmal eine 4 bekomme, wird in meinem Zeugnis eine 2 stehen / werde ich im Zeugnis eine 2 haben.

12. Sonderformen

52 53

Übung 1

1. + e) If you mix red and blue, you get purple. → logische Folge
2. + f) If Julie has finished her homework, she may visit Jackie.
   → Bedingung ist bereits erfüllt worden
3. + b) Laura would be sad if she hadn't made it up with Jonas.
   → Bedingung liegt in der Vergangenheit, die Folge in der Gegenwart
4. + c) If you have to learn your vocabulary, you needn't help me with the washing-up.
   → Verpflichtung in der Gegenwart
5. + d) Sam would have bought lots of presents for Sarah's birthday if he was rich.
   → Bedingung liegt in der Gegenwart, die Folge in der Vergangenheit
6. + a) Don't disturb Dad if he's working. → Bedingung ist im Verlauf

Übung 2

1. Don't interrupt Mum if she is still talking on the phone.
   Bedingung ist im Verlauf / Tätigkeitsverb → Present Progressive *im* if-*Satz*
   Beachte die Stellung von still.
2. If there's no battery in your personal stereo, it doesn't work.
   logische Folge → Simple Present *im Hauptsatz*
3. Mr Parker wouldn't be angry with Sarah now if she hadn't been so lazy.
   Signalwort: now *(→ Folge liegt in der Gegenwart)* → Conditional I *im Hauptsatz*
4. Steve may watch TV if he has already cleaned his room.
   Die Bedingung ist bereits erfüllt worden → Present Perfect *im* if-*Satz*
   Beachte: already *muss hier zwischen dem Hilfsverb* (has) *und dem Vollverb* (cleaned) *stehen*
5. If Vicky's mother can speak two foreign languages, she'll get the job.
   „können" = bestehende Fähigkeit → modales Hilfsverb im if-*Satz*
6. If the Parkers had lots of money, they would have flown to Australia last year.
   Signalwort: last year *(→ Folge liegt in der Vergangenheit)* → Conditional II *im Hauptsatz*

Übung 3

Falls du die Stellung von if-*Satz und Hauptsatz vertauscht hast, ist das selbstverständlich auch richtig!*

1. If you eat too much fast-food, you get fat.
   Hier wird eine logische Folge zum Ausdruck gebracht. Im Hauptsatz steht daher das Simple Present.
   Vorsicht Falle: das deutsche „wird" drückt hier kein Futur aus!
   Beachte die Schreibweise von fast-food *im Englischen!*
2. Julie wouldn't be ill now if she had worn warmer clothes yesterday.
   Nicht vergessen: (Kleidung) tragen heißt wear
3. If you've translated these sentences correctly, you may call yourself a pro.
   Und? Bist du nun ein Profi?
   Die Schwierigkeiten bei der Übersetzung dieses Satzes dürften weniger bei den Verbformen liegen als bei der Verwendung des unbestimmten Artikels (a pro) *und des Adverbs* (correctly, *da sich „richtig" auf ein Verb, nämlich „übersetzen", bezieht).*

Noch ein kleiner Tipp zum Schluss:
Falls du bei der Bearbeitung der Übungen auf weitere grammatikalische Probleme gestoßen bist, die du gerne wiederholen würdest (z. B. Adverbien), bietet dir der Mentor Verlag eine ganze Reihe von geeigneten Lernhilfen!